모조 영작
Mojo English Writing

모조 영작
Mojo English Writing

모조 영작
Mojo English Writing

토마스 안 · 벨라 정 지음

elearntime

자기 의사를 표현하는 마지막 목적은 타인의 생각이나 행동에 변화를 주기 위한 것입니다. 사람을 움직이게 하려면 의미가 강하고 설득적인 표현이어야 합니다. 본서의 제목인 mojo는 대단히 효과적이면서 성공적으로 다른 사람의 주장을 받아들여 움직이게 만드는 마법과도 같은 '강력한 힘'이라는 의미입니다. 다시 말해 모조 영작이란 힘이 살아서 솟구치며 제압하는 듯한 강력하고 설득력 있는 영어 작문이라고 설명할 수 있습니다.

설득되기보다 설득할 수 있는 표현이 무엇인지 생각해 봅니다. 총을 겨눈 전쟁 상황이라면 탄알이 풍부한 편이 오래 버틸 수 있습니다. 탄알은 곧 단어력입니다. 우리말을 영어로 표현하고 싶은데 말이 잘 떠오르지 않는다면 단어의 문제이고, 아는 단어라 하더라도 부적절하게 사용하면 의미가 불분명해지면서 심하면 정반대의 뜻이 될 수 있습니다.

알고 있는 단어를 중심으로 조심스럽게 문장을 만들어보지만 여러 가지 면에서 mojo와 같은 힘있는 표현이 될지 의문이 생깁니다. 다양한 해외 거래를 성공적으로 진행하려면 상대방을 설득해야 하는데 모호하고 적절치 못한 표현은 경쟁력을 허약하게 만들 뿐만 아니라 잘못된 말 또는 문장으로 인해 의도와 달리 오해까지 발생할 수 있습니다.

게다가, 우리나라의 정서를 근거로 하여 표현한 내용이 영미권의 정서에도 똑같이 적용되지 않는 경우 역시 논란이 생길 수 있습니다. 오해를 만들지 않으며 정확한 의사를 주고 받는 영어다운 표현 능력이 필수입니다. 영어에서 정확한 고급 표현이 가능한 단계에 도달하려면 단어는 물론 표현 방법과 문화적 차이에서 오는 감정도 이해해야 합니다.

Mojo English Writing 모조 영작에서는 한글 문장을 이용하여 영어공부를 시작합니다. 왜냐하면 영어를 배우는 목적 자체가 말 또는 글로 된 한글의 의미 전달이기 때문입니다. 본서에는 국내 일간지에 게재된 일상을 표현한 한글 일부를 영어로 옮기는 연습을 합니다. 처음에는 막막할 수 있지만 제시한 문장에 단어를 적용하여 첫 단계의 문장을 만들어 봅니다. practice에서 제시한 문장(완성도 80%내외)의 다른 표현을 보며 suggestion 보충 제안을 참조합니다. 마지막으로 mojo 문장과 비교하며 어떻게 다른지 음미합니다. 이것이 가장 빠른 방법입니다.

학습이라 생각하는 대신 같은 문장에 대한 모델이 될 수 있는 표현을 검토하고 비교하는 mojo 과정은 말할 수 없는 흥미를 일으키고 더 나아가 표현에 관한 영어문화의 새로운 격조와 감동을 느끼게 될 것입니다. 또한 mojo에 수록된 영어 표현들은 가까이 두고 백과사전 식으로 참고할 내용임을 자부합니다. 끝으로 언어 문화에는 법칙이 존재하지 않으므로 문법에 앞서 가급적 시행착오를 거치며 바른 표현 그대로 익히는 것만이 지름길임을 강조하고 싶습니다.

수능을 앞두고 다시 반짝 추위가 찾아왔습니다.

내일은 오늘보다 더 쌀쌀하겠지만,
다행히 모레 수능날에는 추위가 누그러지겠습니다.
자세한 날씨는 야외에 나가있는 기상캐스터를 연결해 알아봅니다.
김민지 캐스터.
네, 저는 지금 덕수궁 돌담길에 나와있습니다.
하늘에서는 가을볕이 내리쬐고 있지만,
바람은 겨울마냥 찹니다.
수능을 코앞에 두고 반짝 추위가 찾아왔기 때문입니다.
수험생들은 마지막까지 감기 걸리지 않도록
건강관리를 잘 해야겠습니다.

text	수능을 앞두고 다시 반짝 추위가 찾아왔습니다
try	[word] 수능 · 수학능력시험 **the College Scholastic Ability Test**
text	내일은 오늘보다 더 쌀쌀하겠지만, 다행히 모레 수능날에는 추위가 누그러지겠습니다.
try	[word] 쌀쌀하다 **chilly · cold** 다행히 **luckily** 누그러지다 **warmer**

Mojo Writing

A cold snap has come just ahead of the college scholastic ability test for students.

Tomorrow will be colder than it is today. Weather forecaster says that the day after tomorrow, test day, it will get mild.
For details of information, we will get back to weather caster who is now on air outdoors.
Hello, is there caster, Kim Minji?
I am around the stone wall at Duksoo Palace.
Well, it is autumn sun shining now, but it is cold like winter.
It is because a flash of cold weather has come right before test taking day.
Students taking the test need to take the best care of their health to the last.

practice	It has come brief cold ahead of the College Scholastic Ability Test ~~on~~ this year. **[Suggestion] Test on this year → Test this year**
mojo	A cold snap has come just ahead of the college scholastic ability test for students. **[tip] cold snap** 일시적 한파 · 갑자기 엄습하는 한기 · 추운 기간 **just ahead** 바로 앞에
practice	Although tomorrow will be colder than today, until the day after tomorrow, at the test day, it will ~~luckily get~~ milder. **[Suggestion] luckily get → get luckily**
mojo	Tomorrow will be colder than it is today. Weather forecaster says that the day after tomorrow, test day, it will get mild. **[tip] than it is today** 오늘 날씨보다 **weather forecaster** 일기예보

text	자세한 날씨는 야외에 나가있는 기상캐스터를 연결해 알아봅니다.
try	[word] 기상캐스터 **weather caster**

text	김민지 캐스터.
try	[word] 기상캐스터 · 기상정보제공자 **caster**

text	네, 저는 지금 덕수궁 돌담길에 나와있습니다.
try	[word] 덕수궁 돌담길 **the stone wall of DukSoo Palace**

text	하늘에서는 가을볕이 내리쬐고 있지만, 바람은 겨울마냥 찹니다.
try	[word] 내리쬐다 **shine down · beat down on**

practice	We are able to get more detail information ~~through~~ a weather caster who is on outdoors. [**Suggestion**] througha weather caster → from a weather caster
mojo	**For details of information, we will get back to weather caster who is now on air outdoors.** [tip] **on air outdoors** 야외 방송중인

practice	Caster Kim Minji.
mojo	**Hello, is there caster, Kim Minji?** [tip] **hello** 여보세요

practice	Yes now, I've come out ~~at~~ the stone wall of DukSoo Palace. [**Suggestion**] **come out at the stone wall → come out to the stone wall**
mojo	**I am around the stone wall at Duksoo Palace.** [tip] **I am around** 근처에 · 주위에 있다

practice	It's beating down autumn sunlit from the sky, while wind is cold ~~winter-like~~. [**Suggestion**] **is cold winter-like → is cold like winter**
mojo	**Well, it is autumn sun shining now, but it is cold like winter.** [tip] **autumn sun shining** 가을 볕이 내리쬐다

수능을 코앞에 두고 반짝 추위가 찾아왔기 때문입니다.

[word] 코앞에 두고 · 바로 전에 **right before**

수험생들은 마지막까지 감기 걸리지 않도록 건강관리를 잘 해야겠습니다.

[word] 수험생들 **test taker** 건강관리 **health care**

practice

~~That's why~~ brief cold weather came here right before the student's test.

[Suggestion] That's why → 원인이 된다는 의미

mojo

It is because a flash of cold weather has come right before the test taking day.

[tip] flash moment 순간포착 **flash idea** 언뜻 떠오른 생각

---

practice

It needs to health care well for the test taker to not get a cold ~~at~~ the test ~~finished~~.

[Suggestion] at the test finished → **until the test to the end**

mojo

Students taking the test need to take the best care of their health to the last.

[tip] students taking the test 시험치는 학생 · 수험생들
to take the best 최선을 다하다

혼자 잠잔다는 것

당신은 누군가와 함께 잠을 자는 것이 온기, 포옹, 로맨스 등으로 더 좋다고
생각하는가? 하지만 밤에 오롯이 당신 혼자만의 공간을 가졌을 때
가질 수 있는 좋은 점도 많다.
몇몇 연구자들은 당신이 침대에서 다른 사람과 함께 자는 것이
사실은 건강에 나쁠 수 있다고 말한다.
특히 수면 상태를 유지하는 부분에 있어서 더욱 그렇다.

text	혼자 잠잔다는 것
try	
	[word] 혼자 alone · single person · by oneself

text	당신은 누군가와 함께 잠을 자는 것이 온기, 포옹, 로맨스 등으로 더 좋다고 생각하는가?
try	
	[word] 온기 **warmth**　포옹 **embrace**　로맨스 **romance**

text	하지만 밤에 오롯이 당신 혼자만의 공간을 가졌을 때 가질 수 있는 좋은 점도 많다.
try	
	[word] 오롯이 **sufficiently·completely·perfectly**　공간을 가지다 **occupy space**

Mojo Writing

What sleeping alone is

Do you think it is true that sleeping with someone may be better with its warmth, embrace and romance? When you occupy your own space alone at night, it may be good itself.
Some of researchers point out that sleeping with other might do bad for health. When it comes to maintaining the good level of sleep, among other things, it could be more so.

practice	What sleeping alone is **[Suggestion] sleeping along** 외롭게 잠자기
mojo	**Sleeping by oneself** **[tip] by oneself** 홀로
practice	Do you think ~~what~~ you sleep with someone has advantage of feeling warm, embracing and romance? **[Suggestion] What(something that) → that**
mojo	**Do you think it is true that sleeping with someone may be better with its warmth, embrace and romance?** **[tip] it is true** 사실이다 **may be better with its warmth** 온기로 더 좋을 지 모른다
practice	But when you occupy ~~your space~~ alone at night, you would have a lot of good point. **[Suggestion] your space → your own space**
mojo	**When you occupy your own space alone at night, it may be good itself.** **[tip] your own space alone** 혼자만의 공간

text

몇몇 연구자들은 당신이 침대에서 다른 사람과 함께 자는 것이 사실은 건강에 나쁠 수 있다고 말한다.

try

[word] 몇몇 연구자들 some of researchers

text

특히 수면 상태를 유지하는 부분에 있어서 더욱 그렇다.

try

[word] 특히 above all 유지 keep

practice

Some of researchers say sleeping together makes ~~worse in health~~ frankly.

[Suggestion] makes worse in health → makes your health bad

mojo

Some of researchers point out that sleeping with other might do bad for health.

[tip] **point out** 언급하다 · 밝히다 · 지적하다

sleeping together 다른 사람과 함께 자다 **do bad for** 나쁘다

---

practice

Above all in a part of keeping sleeping, further so does it.

[Suggestion] above all → above all,

mojo

When it comes to maintaining the good level of sleep, among other things, it could be more so.

[tip] **when it comes to** ～라면 · ～에 관한 한

among other things 그 중에서도 특히

✎

**멋스런 디자인에 실용성 겸비,
'코리 백' 들면 외출이 즐거워진다**

이태리의 감성과 라이프 스타일이 잘 반영된 이태리 가죽 브랜드
헨리베글린은 2016년 가을/겨울 시즌을 맞이해 완벽한 데일리 백이 돼 줄
새로운 라인의 '코리 백'을 선보인다.
심플한 트라페즈 형태로 디자인된 코리백은 탈부착이 가능한
숄더 스트랩이 있어서 크로스백으로 연출할 수도 있으며,
외부에 포켓이 있어서 실용성까지 겸비했다.
시즌과 스타일에 구애 받지 않는 스타일로 가벼우면서도 멋스럽게 들 수 있는
실용적이면서도 스타일리스한 백으로 전국의 헨리베글린 매장에서
만나볼 수 있다.

text	멋스런 디자인에 실용성 겸비, '코리 백' 들면 외출이 즐거워진다
try	
	[word] 멋스런 디자인 **fancy design** 실용성 · 실용적인 도움이 되는 **useful** 부풀어오르다 **puff up**

03

Mojo Writing

With a combination of elegance and practicality, carrying Cori bag makes outgoing joyful.

Henry Beguelin, Italian leather brand, reflecting a good mix of Italian sensibility and lifestyle, is going to put out a new line of Cori bag, which they hope will become a perfect bag for daily use facing 2016 autumn/ winter season.

Cori bag, designed with simple trapeze shape, may serve as a crossing bag with a detachable shoulder strap and give even practical use with attached outpocket to it.

Along with its style free from season and style, the bag is useful and stylish feeling light and fancy to carry. Now is time when you can meet Henry Beguelin stores across this country.

practice

Thanks to useful and fancy design, you are puffed up ~~as~~ going out carrying Cori bag.

[Suggestion] as→ when

mojo

With a combination of elegance and practicality, carrying Cori bag makes going outjoyful.

[tip] **combination** 결합 · 복합 **elegance** 우아함 · 고상함 **practicality** 실용성

text

이태리의 감성과 라이프 스타일이 잘 반영된 이태리 가죽 브랜드 헨리베글린은 2016년 가을/겨울 시즌을 맞이해 완벽한 데일리 백이 돼 줄 새로운 라인의 '코리 백'을 선보인다.

try

[word] 감성 **emotions**　반영하다 **refect influence**　헨리 베글린 **Henry Beguelin**
데일리백 **daily bag**　선보이다 **show**

---

text

심플한 트라페즈 형태로 디자인된 코리백은 탈부착이 가능한 숄더 스트랩이 있어서 크로스백으로 연출할 수도 있으며, 외부에 포켓이 있어서 실용성까지 겸비했다.

try

[word] 트라페즈 · 사다리꼴 **trapeze**　탈부착 **removable · attachable · detach able**　숄더 스트랩 · 어깨에 매는 끈 **shoulder strap**　크로스백 **cross bag**　겸비하다
combine

practice

Henry Beguelin, one of leather bag company famous for expressing Italic emotions and lifestyles, shows Cori bags of new line that will be perfect daily bag this SS seasons in 2016.

mojo

Henry Beguelin, Italian leather brand, reflecting a good mix of Italian sensibility and lifestyle, is going to put out a new line of Cori bag, which they hope will become a perfect bag for daily use facing 2016 autumn/ winter season.

[tip] **leather brand** 가죽제품 회사 **reflecting a good mix of** 혼합을 잘 반영한 **put out** 출시하다 · 꺼내보이다

---

practice

~~Cori bag designed~~ simple trapeze shape can be expressed a crossing bag with a detachable shoulder strap and use a practical bag by attaching outpocket.

[Suggestion] **Cori bag designed → Cori bag, designed**

mojo

Cori bag, designed with simple trapeze shape, may serve as a crossing bag with a detachable shoulder strap and give even practical use with attached outpocket to it.

[tip] **trapeze shape** 사다리꼴 형태 **may serve as a crossing bag** 크로스백으로 연출할 수도 있다 **even plactical use** 실용성까지

시즌과 스타일에 구애 받지 않는 스타일로 가벼우면서도 멋스럽게 들 수 있는 실용적이면서도 스타일리스한 백으로 전국의 헨리베글린 매장에서 만나볼 수 있다.

[word] 구애 받지 않는 · 상관없이 · 무관하게 **regardless**

<table>
<tr><td>practice</td><td>With the style regardless season and style, it becomes useful and stylish bag feeling of light and fancy and you are able to meet <del>with</del> it every Henry Beguelin Store in whole country.
[Suggestion] to meet with it → to meet it</td></tr>
<tr><td>mojo</td><td>Along with its style free from season and style, the bag is useful and stylish feeling light and fancy to carry. Now is time when you can meet Henry Beguelin stores across this country.
[tip] along with 함께 · 더불어 · 따라 free from 자유로운 · 구애없이 feeling light and fancy to carry 들기에 가벼우면서도 멋스럽게 now is time when 지금은 이런 때</td></tr>
</table>

트럼프 당선 예언

영화감독 마이클 무어의 "사이코패스 트럼프가 대통령에 당선될 것이라는
다섯 가지 족집게 예언이 화제다.
다섯 번째, 제시 벤추라 효과를 들었다. 프로레슬러 출신인 벤추라는 1998년
미네소타 주지사에 당선된 인물이다.
과거 벤추라를 뽑았을 때처럼 사람들이 병든 정치 시스템에 대한
분노의 표시로 트럼프를 뽑는
장난을 칠 것이라고 무어는 지적했다

text	트럼프 당선 예언
try	[word] 트럼프 **Trump**　당선 **elect**　예언 **prediction** · **foretell**
text	영화감독 마이클 무어의 "사이코패스 트럼프가 대통령에 당선될 것이라는 다섯 가지 족집게 예언이 화제다.
try	[word] 영화감독 **film director**　족집게 · 콕 집다 **pin** 사이코패스 · 정신병자 · 변질자 **psychopath**　예언 **forecast**
text	다섯번째, 제시 벤추라 효과를 들었다.
try	[word] 제시 벤추라 **Jesse Ventura**

04

The predition of Trump winning

Five pinpointing predictions by film director, Michael Francis
Moore, that a psychopath, Trump will be elected president, are
now the popular talk of the town.
In the fifth instance, he cited the effect of Ventura. Ventura, then
a pro wrestler, was elected Minnesota governor in 1998. Moore
pointed out that, like people chose Ventura in the past, they would
elect Trump in fun as a sign of their bursting anger against the
ailing political and social system.

practice	The prediction of Trump winning
mojo	**The prediction of Trump winning**

practice	Pinned five forecasts by a film director Michael Francis Moore are now issued: "The psychopath, Trump will be elected as a new president."
mojo	**Five pinpointing predictions by film director, Michael Francis Moore, that a psychopath, Trump will be elected president, are now the popular talk of the town.**

[tip] **pinpoint** 정확한 · 정확한 지적 **prediction** 예상
talk of the town 장안의 화제

practice	Fifth is raised an effect of Jesse Ventura.
mojo	**In the fifth instance, he cited the effect of Ventura.**

[tip] **instance** 예 · 사례 · 일례 **cite** 말하다 · 예로 들다

text	프로레슬러 출신인 벤추라는 1998년 미네소타 주지사에 당선된 인물이다.
try	
	[word] 미네소타 주지사 **Minnesota Governor**

text	과거 벤추라를 뽑았을 때처럼 사람들이 병든 정치 시스템에 대한 분노의 표시로 트럼프를 뽑는 장난을 칠 것이라고 무어는 지적했다.
try	
	[word] 병든 정치 시스템 **ailing political system** 장난 · 악영향 · 곤란한 일 **mischief**

<table>
<tr><td>practice</td><td>He was elected as Minnesota Governor in 1998 from a professional wrestler.</td></tr>
<tr><td>mojo</td><td>Ventura, then a pro wrestler, was elected Minnesota governor in 1998.</td></tr>
</table>

[tip] **then a pro wrestler** 당시 프로레슬러

<table>
<tr><td>practice</td><td>Moor pointed out that people would make a mischief by choosing him as a bursting of rage against ailing political system like choose Ventura in past.</td></tr>
<tr><td>mojo</td><td>Moore pointed out that, like people chose Ventura in the past, they would elect Trump in fun as a sign of their bursting anger against the ailing political and social system.</td></tr>
</table>

[tip] **point out** 지적하다 **their bursting anger** 그들의 분노 분출

아 랑에 운트 죄네

아 랑에 운트 죄네는 오직 골드와 플래티넘 등의 고급 소재만을 사용해
연간 단 몇 천 점 내외의 워치만을 한정적으로 제작합니다.
제품에 사용된 무브먼트 역시 브랜드 고유의 섬세한 수공기술로
화려하게 장식되고 조립되어 아 랑에 운트 죄네만의 특별함을 더합니다.
약 200여 년간 아 랑에 운트 죄네는 51개의 메뉴팩쳐 칼리버를 개발하여
전세계 하이앤드 워치 브랜드 중 최고의 위치를 고수하고 있습니다.

text	제품에 사용된 무브먼트 역시 브랜드 고유의 섬세한 수공기술로 화려하게 장식되고 조립되어 아 랑에 운트 죄네만의 특별함을 더합니다.
try	

[word] 무브먼트 · 움직임 · 변화 **movement** 수공기술 **handicraft**
장식되고 조립되다 **decorative and assemble**

text	아 랑에 운트 죄네는 오직 골드와 플래티넘 등의 고급 소재만을 사용해 연간 단 몇 천 점 내외의 워치만을 한정적으로 제작합니다.
try	

[word] 아 랑에 운트 죄네 **A. Lange &Söhne** 플래티넘 · 백금 **platinum**

05

The A. Lange & Söhne

The A. Lange & Söhne makes limited thousands of watches a year using only gold and high quality of platinum. The movements used in the products are trimmed and assembled colorfully with a unique delicacy, adding specialty only the A. Lange & Söhne deserve. Over past 200 years, the A. Lange & Söhne developed 51 manufactural calibers and still hold an unchallenged position in global top watch brands.

practice	The A. Lange & Söhne (Germany) has been made limited thousands watches a year using only gold and high quality platinum.
mojo	**The A. Lange & Söhne makes limited thousands of watches a year using only gold and high quality of platinum.** [tip] **make limited** 한정적으로 만들다
practice	Using unique and delicate handicraft art at details of movements has also added to specialty of decorative effect glamorously and assembles on products.
mojo	**The movements used in the products are trimmed and assembled colorfully with a unique delicacy, adding specialty only the A. Lange & Söhne deserve.** [tip] **trimmed and assembled** 다듬어지고 조립되다 **deserve** 만하다 · 가치

약 200여 년간 아 랑에 운트 죄네는 51개의 메뉴팩쳐 칼리버를 개발하여 전세계 하이앤드 워치 브랜드 중 최고의 위치를 고수하고 있습니다.

[word] 메뉴팩쳐칼리버 · 제조역량 · 품질측정도구 **manufactural caliber**

practice

During historical about 200 years, A. Lange & Söhne has developed 51 manufactural calibers and then has still made top watches among high-end brands of all ~~of~~ the world.

[Suggestion] allof the world → all over the world

mojo

Over past 200 years, the A. Lange & Söhne developed 51 manufactural calibers and still hold an unchallenged position in global top watch brands.

[tip] over past 과거에 걸쳐서 **still hold** 고수하다
unchallenged position 최고의 위치

타임랩스 기법

지난 12일 최순실 게이트가 촉발한 국기문란 사태에 분노한 시민들로부터
100만여 촛불이 타오른 가운데 그날의 함성을 타임랩스 기법으로 기록한 영상이
화제가 되고 있다.
타임랩스는 일정하게 정해진 간격으로 움직임을 저속 촬영한 뒤
이를 정상속도로 영사하는 특수 영상기법이다.
시민 오정환씨가 6000여 장을 촬영해 이를 한편의 영상으로 만들어 보내온
타임랩스 영상을 공개한다.

text

지난 12일 최순실 게이트가 촉발한 국기문란 사태에 분노한 시민들로부터
100만여 촛불이 타오른 가운데 그날의 함성을 타임랩스 기법으로 기록한
영상이 화제가 되고 있다.

try

[word] 국기문란 **national disorder** 함성 **chanting**
타임랩스 · 저속촬영기법 **timelapse cinematography**

06

Mojo Writing

Timelapse skill

On November 12, more than one million people protested against Chwey Soonsil scandal, holding candlelight vigil to show their rage. Their outcry has been published using Timelapse cinematography with a public attention.

Timelapse skill is a special one that captures movement of object in a slow speed on basis of regular interval and projects the clip on the screen at normal speed.

We make a video public, which a Korean citizen, Mr. Oh Jungwhan has made himself after shooting about 6000 clips.

practice   On November 12, amid million candles being bringing from raged people caused by ChweySoonsil gate flamed, a recoded chanting video using Timelapse cinematography at the day is issued.

mojo   On November 12, more than one million people protested against Chwey Soonsil scandal, holding candlelight vigil to show their rage. Their outcry has been published using Timelapse cinematography with a public attention.

[tip] **candlelight vigil** 철야 촛불 **rage** 분노 **outcry** 함성 · 격렬한 항의

text	타임랩스는 일정하게 정해진 간격으로 움직임을 저속 촬영한 뒤 이를 정상속도로 영사하는 특수 영상기법이다.
try	

[word] 정해진 간격 **settled regular interval** 정상속도 **norm speed** 영상 **clip**

text	시민 오정환 씨가 6000여장을 촬영해 이를 한편의 영상으로 만들어 보내온 타임랩스 영상을 공개한다.
try	

[word] 시민 **citizen** 영상 **image**

practice

Timelapse skill is a kind of special techniques that ~~is taking~~ some movements by ~~low~~ speed settled regular intervals and then turns norm clip.

[Suggestion] thatis taking some → that takes some by low speed → by slow speed

mojo

Timelapse skill is a special one that captures movement of object in a slow speed on basis of regular interval and projects the clip on the screen at normal speed.

[tip] object 대상 **on basis of regular interval** 일정하게 정해진 간격으로

---

practice

We make it ~~in~~ public that given us the image which citizen Oh Jungwhan has made one of video after taking more than 6000 photos

[Suggestion] makeit in public → make it public

mojo

We make a video public, which a Korean citizen, Mr. Oh JungWhan has made himself after shooting about 6000 clips.

[tip] shooting 촬영하다

공기청정기 대신 이끼화분… 엄마 마음 잡은 '플랜테리어'(식물 인테리어)

가습기 살균제를 시작으로 공기청정기 필터 논란 등
화학제품의 안전성을 둘러싼 불안 탓에
케미포비아(화학제품 공포증)가
우리 사회 전반에 확산하고 있다.
이런 흐름을 타고 식물을 인테리어 소품 삼아
자연스럽게 건강까지 챙기는 플렌테리어(planterior)가 관심을 모은다.
플랜테리어는 식물을 뜻하는 플랜트와 실내장식을 의미하는
인테리어(interior)를 합친 단어다.
특히 올해는 중국발 미세먼지·초미세먼지 농도가 더 짙어진 탓에
공기 정화 효과가 있는 식물에 대한 관심이 더욱 높아지고 있다.

text	공기청정기 대신 이끼화분… 엄마 마음 잡은 '플랜테리어'(식물 인테리어)
try	

[word] 공기청정기 **air cleaner**　이끼화분 **a vase of moss**　플랜테리어 **planterior**

07

With a combination of elegance and practicality, carrying Cori bag makes outgoing joyful.

Moss flowerpot for air purifier, planterior has occupied moms' mind. With the apprehension about the safety of chemical products, including the controversy over the air purifier filter to begin with humidifier sterilizer, chemo phobia is spreading through our societies at large. Riding over the wave, the planterior is attracting public attention, keeping health in a natural way with adoption of the plant as props.

Planterior is a compound word of a word meaning plant and interior defining interior ornament. Especially this year the concentration of both fine dust and superfine dust out of China is getting thicker, and so the public attention on the plant having purification effect on air is getting much more higher.

practice	The mind of mother is held by planterior(plant interior) choosing such as a vase of moss ~~instead of~~ an air cleaner. **[Suggestion] instead of → for**
mojo	Moss flowerpot for air purifier, planterior has occupied moms' mind. **[tip] flowerpot** 화분 **air purifier** 공기정화기 **occupy** 차지하다 · 들어서다

text

가습기 살균제를 시작으로 공기청정기 필터 논란 등 화학제품의 안전성을
둘러싼 불안 탓에 케미포비아(화학제품 공포증)가 우리 사회 전반에 확산하고
있다.

try

[word] 가습기 살균제 **humidifier sterilizer**
케미포비아 · 화학제품 공포증 **chemophobia**

---

text

이런 흐름을 타고 식물을 인테리어 소품 삼아 자연스럽게 건강까지 챙기는
플렌테리어(planterior)가 관심을 모은다.

try

[word] 소품 **properties** 관심 **interest**

---

text

플랜테리어는 식물을 뜻하는 플랜트와 실내장식을 의미하는 인테리어를
합친 단어다.

try

[word] 식물 **plant** 실내장식을 의미하는 인테리어 **a word meaning interior**

practice

With concern~~ing~~ about starting the humidifier sterilizers, controversies of air cleaner filter, and over security of chemicals, chemophobia is getting spread across our societies.

[Suggestion] concerning about → concern about

mojo

With the apprehension about the safety of chemical products, including the controversy over the air purifier filter to begin with humidifier sterilizer, chemo phobia is spreading through our societies at large.

[tip] apprehension 불안·걱정 **to begin with** 우선 **at large** 전반적으로

---

practice

This situation follows that planterior ~~is~~ drew people's interest to interior of a property planting adding their health as a result.

[Suggestion] that planterior is drew → that planterior drew

mojo

Riding over the wave, the planterior is attracting public attention, keeping health in a natural way with adoption of the plant as props.

[tip] ride over the wave 이런 흐름을 타고 **is attracting** 관심을 모은다 **in a natural way** 자연스럽게 **props** 소품·소도구

---

practice

Planterior means word 'plant' combined with decorative 'interior.'

mojo

Planterior is a compound word of a word meaning plant and interior defining interior ornament.

[tip] a compound word 합친단어·복합단어 **ornament** 장식

특히 올해는 중국발 미세먼지·초미세먼지 농도가 더 짙어진 탓에
공기 정화 효과가 있는 식물에 대한 관심이 더욱 높아지고 있다.

[word] 미세먼지·초미세먼지 **fine and ultra-fine dust**

This year, since especially it is thicker fine and ultra-fine dust from China, plants in which has effect ~~of~~ air clear are getting higher attention to people.

[Suggestion] effect of air → effect on air

Especially this year the concentration of both fine dust and superfine dust out of China is getting thicker, and so the public attention on the plant having purification effect on air is getting much more higher.

[tip] out of China 중국발 purification effect 정화효과

태양의 나라 멕시코

선인장과 프리다 칼로, 마리아치와 루차 리브레, 사파티스타와
죽음의 날, 데낄라와 코로나, 정열의 나라 멕시코에는 무지개 빛깔보다
많은 아이콘들이 있습니다.
여러 아이콘 중에서도 가장 먼저 떠오르는 것은 데낄라입니다.
누구나 데낄라에 대한 사연 한 가지쯤 품고 있을 것 같아요.
손등에 소금을 올리고 혀로 살짝 소금 맛을 본 후, 잔을 탁자에 탁탁 두드리고
식도를 열어 단숨에 들이키는 데낄라. 데낄라가 뜨거운 사랑의 맛이라면
그 사랑이 주는 상처를 치유하는 것은 레몬의 몫입니다.
그래서 데낄라가 주는 짜릿함을 맛본 후에는 준비한 레몬을
얼른 입에 물어야 합니다

text

선인장과 프리다 칼로, 마리아치와 루차 리브레, 사파티스타와 죽음의 날,
데낄라와 코로나, 정열의 나라 멕시코에는 무지개 빛깔보다 많은 아이콘들이
있습니다.

try

[word] 선인장 **cactus** 프리다 칼로 · 멕시코 화가 **Frida kahol's Paintings**
마리아치 · 멕시코 음악 **mariachi** 루차 리브레 · 멕시코 레슬링 **Lucha libre**
사파티스타와 죽음의 날 · 혁명의 날 **Zapatista, Día de Muertos**
데낄라와 코로나 · 멕시코 술과 맥주 **Tequila and Corona**

08

Mexico, Solar Nation

Cactus, Frida Kahlos paintings Mariachi, Lucha libre, Zapatist Tequila de Dias de Muertos, Mexico, the nation of passion, boasts more icons than the color of rainbow. What occurs to mind firs among many icons, is Tequila.

It may be as if everyone would entertain more than one episode about Tequila. Tasting lightly salt on the back of hand, flapping a cup on the table and gulping tequila into open gullet, while Tequila teaches what love is like, lemon heals the scar of the love. That's why you need to hold fast the lemon in your mouth right after tasting the pungent taste of Tequila.

practice Cactus, Frida Kahlo's Paintings, Mariachi, Lucha libre, Zapatista, Día de Muertos, Tequila and Corona, Mexico, the nation of passion, has abundance icons, say it is more than the color of rainbow.

mojo Cactus, Frida Kahlos paintings, Mariachi, Lucha libre, Zapatist Tequila de Dias de Muertos, Tequila and Corona, Mexico, the nation of passion, boasts more icons than the color of rainbow.

[tip] **boast** 가지고 있다 · 자랑하다 · 내세우다

text	여러 아이콘 중에서도 가장 먼저 떠오르는 것은 데낄라입니다. 누구나 데낄라에 대한 사연 한 가지쯤 품고 있을 것 같아요.
try	

[word] 아이콘 **icon**　가장 먼저 **first of all**　(마음 속에) 떠오르다 **occurs to mind**

text	손등에 소금을 올리고 혀로 살짝 소금 맛을 본 후, 잔을 탁자에 탁탁 두드리고 식도를 열어 단숨에 들이키는 데낄라. 데낄라가 뜨거운 사랑의 맛이라면 그 사랑이 주는 상처를 치유하는 것은 레몬의 몫입니다.
try	

[word] 손등 **back of your hand**　두드리다 **tap**　식도 **gullet**　들이키다 **gulp**
상처 **hurt**　치유 **heal**

text	그래서 데낄라가 주는 짜릿함을 맛본 후에는 준비한 레몬을 얼른 입에 물어야 합니다.
try	

[word] 짜릿하다 **piquant**

| **practice** | Everybody may keep at least a story over Tequila in their heart. |
| **mojo** | What occurs to mind first among many icons, is Tequila. It may be as if everyone would entertain more than one episode about Tequila. |

[tip] it may be as if ~일 것이다 **entertain** 마음에 품다 **episode** 사연

---

practice

Try Tequila this way: leak and taste lightly a bit salt on ~~putting~~ the back ofyour hand, and then gulp down the Tequila at once into opening gullet after tapping on the table. While Tequila gives taste of burning love, what heals the hurt of love is owed lemon.

[Suggestion] on putting the back of your hand → on the back of your hand

mojo

Tasting lightly salt on the back of hand, flapping a cup on the table and gulping tequila into open gullet, while Tequila teaches what love is like, lemon heals the scar of the love.

[tip] flapping a cup 잔을 탁탁 두드리고 **the scar of the love** 사랑의 상처

---

practice

That's why you need bite prepared a piece of lemon after tasting a sense of piquant giving Tequila.

[Suggestion] bite 물다

mojo

That's why you need to hold fast the lemon in your mouth right after tasting the pungent taste of Tequila.

[tip] pungent taste 짜릿한 맛

부동산시장 전망

엎친 데 덮친 격이다. 11·3 부동산대책으로
한파를 맞은 서울 강남 재건축시장에 이번엔 난기류가 몰아치고 있다.
반포·잠실 일대 굵직한 재건축단지의 사업계획이
서울시 문턱을 넘지 못해서다.
가뜩이나 매수세가 꺾인 상황에서 재건축사업 추진에도 브레이크가 걸리면서
시장이 더욱 움츠러드는 양상이다.
17일 서울시에 따르면 전날 도시계획위원회는
반포 주공 1단지 정비계획을 심의했으나 결론을 못 내고 보류시켰다.
지난 7월에 이어 두 번째 보류 결정이다.

text	부동산시장 전망
try	[word] 부동산 **realty** · **real estate**　전망 **prospect** · **view**
text	엎친 데 덮친 격이다.
try	[word] 엎치다 **turn over**　덮치다 **hold down** · **raid** · **press down**

09

Mojo Writing

The market of real estate

Matters have gone from bad to worse. The market of apartments to be rebuilt in Ghangnam, hit by the crisis of 11·3 real estate measure, is being swept over by severe turbulence this time.
The housing project of some large reconstruction complex in Banpo and Jamsil area did not cross the threshold of Seoul City.
On the top of buying power being subsided, the business of reconstruction has been on sharp decline, and shrank back in the uncertain prospect of the market.
According to Seoul City announcement, the City Committee deliberated the developing of Banpo Jugong 1 complex, but on hold without any conclusion. It is second decision on hold since last July.

practice	The prospect of realty market
mojo	**The market of real estate**
	[tip] market 시장 · 시장경기 · 시세

practice	This situation couldn't be worse.
	[Suggestion] →상황이 이보다 더 나쁠 수 없다 (본 의미에 차이가 있다)
mojo	**Matters have gone from bad to worse.**
	[tip] matters 문제 · 일 · 사건

text

11·3 부동산대책으로 한파를 맞은 서울 강남 재건축시장에 이번엔 난기류가 몰아치고 있다.

try

[word] 부동산대책 **the measures of real estate** 한파 **cold wave**
난기류 **turbulence**

text

반포·잠실 일대 굵직한 재건축단지의 사업계획이 서울시 문턱을 넘지 못해서다.

try

[word] 아파트단지 **complex** 문턱 **threshold** 넘어가다 **go over**

text

가뜩이나 매수세가 꺾인 상황에서 재건축사업 추진에도 브레이크가 걸리면서 시장이 더욱 움츠러드는 양상이다.

try

[word] 가뜩이나 **moreover** 매수세 **bullish sentiment**

Some air turbulence hit at the reconstruction market in Ghangnam, Seoul getting iced by the measures of real estate on November 3.

mojo

The market of apartments to be rebuilt in Ghangnam, hit by the crisis of 11·3 real estate measures, is being swept over by severe turbulence this time.

[tip] **market of apartments to be rebuilt** 재건될 아파트 시장 **swept over** 몰아치다

---

practice

The housing plan ~~of reconstruction large complex~~ in Banpo and Jamsil area didn't go over the threshold of Seoul city.

[Suggestion] of reconstruction large complex → large complex of reconstruction

mojo

The housing project of some large reconstruction complex in Banpo and Jamsil area did not cross the threshold of Seoul City.

[tip] **housing project** 공영주택단지 · 아파트단지 **cross** 넘다 · 건너다

---

practice

Moreover, in the dropped bullish sentiment of the market, the business of reconstruction has been hooked a break and more squeezed in market.

mojo

On the top of buying power being subsided, the business of reconstruction has been on sharp decline, and shrank back in the uncertain prospect of the market.

[tip] **buying power** 매수세 **subside** 가라앉다
sharp decline 급감 · 쇠퇴 **shank back** 움츠러들다

17일 서울시에 따르면 전날 도시계획위원회는 반포 주공 1단지 정비계획을 심의했으나 결론을 못 내고 보류시켰다.

[word] 정비계획 **developing plan** 심의 **review** 보류 · 연기 **postpone**

지난 7월에 이어 두 번째 보류 결정이다.

[word] 이어서 **following**

| **practice** | According Seoul city on November 17, the city plan committee reviewed the developing plan for Banpo 1 complex at a day earlier, but postponed it without any result after the next day. |

[Suggestion] According Seoul city → According to Seoul city

| **mojo** | **According to Seoul City announcement, the City Committee deliberated the developing of Banpo Jugong 1 complex, but on hold without any conclusion.** |

[tip] according to Seoul City announcement 서울시 발표에 따르면
deliberate 심의하다 **on hold** 보류되다

| **practice** | It is second decision ~~holding~~ for the plan following last July. |

[Suggestion] holding → on hold

| **mojo** | **It is second decision on hold since last July.** |

[tip] since last July 지난 **7**월 이래 **on hold** 보류

주요 안과 질환 예방법

"몸이 천 냥이면 눈은 구백 냥"이라는 속담이 있다.
신체 장기 중 눈이 가장 중요한 기관임을 강조한 말이다.
하지만 요즘 한국인의 눈 건강은 그리 좋은 편이 아니다.
스마트폰·컴퓨터 작업 등으로 혹사당하고,
당뇨병·고혈압 등 만성질환이 안구 혈관까지 망가뜨려
실명에 까지 이르는 사람이 늘고 있다.
서울 성모병원 안과 주천기 교수는
"안구세포는 한번 나빠지면 대부분 돌이킬 수 없어 예방이 무엇보다 중요하다"고
말한다.
한국인의 주요 안과 질환과 예방법을 알아봤다.
망막은 수정체 뒤에 위치한 기관인데, 사진기에 비유하면 필름에 해당한다.
수정체(렌즈)를 통해 들어온 사물의 상이 맺히는 곳이다.
좋은 렌즈를 갖고 있어도 필름에 문제가 있으면
인화된 사진이 잘 보이지 않는 것처럼 망막에 문제가 생기면
사물이 흐려지거나 일그러져 보인다.

text	주요 안과 질환 예방법
try	[word] 안과 질환 ophthalmological disease 예방 prevention
text	"몸이 천 냥이면 눈은 구백 냥"이라는 속담이 있다.
try	[word] 속담 old saying · proverb

Mojo Writing

The prevention method of main ophthalmological disease

There goes an old saying that the eye is valued at 900 cents while the body valued at 1,000 cents. It accentuates that the eye is most important organ in our body. But we deem that eyes of Korean local people are not quite good. They have been driven hard by smart phone and computer, and diabetes or high blood pressure and the chronic diseases have ruined blood vessel, leading to losing their eyesight. Professor Joo Chungi, the Department of Ophthalmology, Seoul the St. Mary's Hospital, says "once eyeball cell deteriorates, it becomes irreversible, noting that prevention matters still more. We have looked to main ophthalmological diseases and the way of prevention.

The retina is an organ located behind the crystalline lens, and it compares to photography film, where the image of object passing through the crystalline lens is being focused on. Like any problem of film with good quality lens produces a blurred photograph, when the retina has any problem with it, you can have bleary eyes in distortion.

practice	The prevention way of ophthalmological disease
mojo	**The prevention method of main ophthalmological disease**

practice	An old saying goes "where is a body for one thousand, eyes are nine hundreds."
mojo	**There goes an old saying that the eye is valued at 900 cents while the body valued at 1,000 cents.**
	[tip] is valued at 가치가 있다 **while** 한편

text

신체 장기 중 눈이 가장 중요한 기관임을 강조한 말이다.

try

[word] 장기 **organ** 강조하다 **emphasize**

text

하지만 요즘 한국인의 눈 건강은 그리 좋은 편이 아니다.

try

[word] 눈 건강 **eye-health**

text

스마트폰 · 컴퓨터작업 등으로 혹사당하고, 당뇨병 · 고혈압 등 만성질환이
안구 혈관까지 망가뜨려 실명에 까지 이르는 사람이 늘고 있다.

try

[word] 혹사 **hard work** 당뇨병 **diabetes** 고혈압 **hypertension**
안구 **eyeball** 실명 **lose one's eyesight**

practice	It emphasizes eye is the most important organ ~~among~~ body's ones. **[Suggestion] among → in**
mojo	**It accentuates that the eye is most important organ in our body.** **[tip] accentuate** 강조하다

practice	But recently Korean's eyes have been ~~ill-health~~. **[Suggestion] ill-health →** 질환을 갖고 있는 · 상태가 나쁜
mojo	**But we deem that eyes of Korean local people are not quite good.** **[tip] We deem that** 우리는 생각한다 · 여기다 **Korean local people** 한국인 **notquite good** 그리좋지 않다

practice	It is getting harder worked through using smart phone or computer, and has broken by diabetes or hypertension and then some people have reached to losing their eyesight. **[Suggestion] has broken their eyesight and then some people have reached to losing by diabetes or hypertension**
mojo	**They have been driven hard by smart phone and computer, and diabetes or high blood pressure and the chronic diseases have ruined blood vessel, leading to losing their eyesight.** **[tip] drive hard** 혹사에 몰리다 **high blood pressure** 고혈압 **ruin** 망치다 **lead to** 이르다

<table>
<tr><td>text</td><td>서울 성모병원 안과 주천기 교수는 "안구세포는 한번 나빠지면 대부분 돌이킬 수 없어 예방이 무엇보다 중요하다"고 말한다.</td></tr>
<tr><td>try</td><td></td></tr>
</table>

[word] 안과 **the Department of Ophthalmology** 돌이키다 **get back**

<table>
<tr><td>text</td><td>한국인의 주요 안과 질환과 예방법을 알아봤다.</td></tr>
<tr><td>try</td><td></td></tr>
</table>

[word] 예방법 **the way of prevention**

<table>
<tr><td>text</td><td>망막은 수정체 뒤에 위치한 기관인데, 사진기에 비유하면 필름에 해당한다.</td></tr>
<tr><td>try</td><td></td></tr>
</table>

[word] 망막 **retina** 수정체 **crystalline lens**

<table>
<tr><td>practice</td><td>Professor Joo chungi, the Department of Ophthalmology Sungmo Hospital, Seoul, said "prevention is essential for keeping eye <s>health</s> because there is almost no way to get back original its sight, once eyeball cells get worse."
[Suggestion] for keeping eye health → for keeping eye healthy</td></tr>
<tr><td>mojo</td><td>Professor Joo Chungi, the Department of Ophthalmology, Seoul the St. Mary's Hospital, says "once eyeball cell deteriorates, it becomes irreversible, noting that prevention matters still more.
[tip] the St. Mary's Hospital 성모병원 deteriorate 악화되다
irreversible 뒤집을 수 없는</td></tr>
</table>

<table>
<tr><td>practice</td><td><s>Review</s> main ophthalmological disease and the way of prevention.
[Suggestion] Review → Review is</td></tr>
<tr><td>mojo</td><td>We have looked to main ophthalmological diseases and the way of prevention.
[tip] look to 유의하다 · 주의를 돌리다</td></tr>
</table>

<table>
<tr><td>practice</td><td>The retina is an organ behind the crystalline lens, a kind of film applying to camera, where focuses imaginal lights of object through the crystalline lens.</td></tr>
<tr><td>mojo</td><td>The retina is an organ located behind the crystalline lens, and it compares to photography film, where the image of object passing through the crystalline lens is being focused on.
[tip] an organ located behind the crystalline lens 수정체 뒤에 위치한 기관</td></tr>
</table>

수정체(렌즈)를 통해 들어온 사물의 상이 맺히는 곳이다. 좋은 렌즈를 갖고 있어도 필름에 문제가 있으면 인화된 사진이 잘 보이지 않는 것처럼 망막에 문제가 생기면 사물이 흐려지거나 일그러져 보인다.

[word] 인화된 사진 **printed photo** 흐려지거나 일그러져 **blurred or twisted**

Whatever has a good lens, if film has problems, its printed photos are likely hard to see. Like this way, where the retina has problems, objects seem to be seen blurred or twisted.

Like any problem of film with good quality lens produces a blurred photograph, when the retina has any problem with it, you can have bleary eyes in distortion.

[tip] **bleary** 흐린 · 흐릿한 **in distortion** 찌그러져

✏️

배만한 배꼽

은행 가산금리 해도 너무해

코픽스(자금조달비용지수) 내려도 가산금리는 상승
은행 '트럼플레이션' 이유 대지만
가계빚 억제 명분으로 배 불리기
대출자 부담 우려, 당국 점검나서
은행권 주택담보대출의 가산금리 상승세가 심상찮다.
하반기 들어 오름폭이 커지더니
이젠 배(기준금리)와 배꼽(가산금리)의 크기가 별 차이가 없다.
대출자의 부담이 커진다는 우려가 나오자
금융감독당국이 점검에 나섰다.

text	배만한 배꼽 은행 가산금리 해도 너무해
try	
	[word] 배꼽 **navel**　가산금리 **additional interest**
text	코픽스내려도 가산금리는 상승
try	
	[word] 코픽스(자금조달비용지수) **COFIX** · **Cost of Funds Index**

11

Mojo Writing

The navel as big as its belly.
The banks' additional interest rate is like going too far.

COFIX down, but additional interest rate is rising up.
The bank gives a reason that it comes from Trumplation, but it just lines its own pocket on the grounds that they want to curb household debts.
The authorities is out to look into market in the fear of expanding the individual debtor' liability.
It is serious concern that the commercial banks' interest rate are moving up.
As the ratio of rising has become wide in the second half of this year, now there is barely difference between the key rate and the additional interest rate.
The Financial Supervisory Commission has come to examine the situation following the fear that debtors'burden would grow.

practice	The commercial banks in Korea are running overly their additional interest systems, just small part like a navel, as a belly.
mojo	The navel as big as its belly… The banks' additional interest rate is like going too far. **[tip] navel is like its belly** 배 같은 배꼽 **additional interest rate · overdue payment** 가산금리
practice	Nevertheless the COFIX downs, it is going up.
mojo	COFIX down, but additional interest rate is rising up. **[tip] is rising up** 오르고 있다

text	은행 '트럼플레이션' 이유 대지만 가계빚 억제 명분으로 배 불리기
try	[word] 트럼플레이션 Trumpflation · Trump+Inflation 가계빚 household debt
text	대출자 부담 우려, 당국 점검나서
try	[word] 당국 authority 점검 check · inspection
text	은행권 주택담보대출의 가산금리 상승세가 심상찮다.
try	[word] 주택담보대출 housing mortgage loan · home equity loan · personal mortgage loan

| **practice** | Although Banks put one of its excuses on 'Trumpflation', it is aiming to burgeon their profit ~~with~~ the ground as curbing house debt. |

[Suggestion] with the ground → on the grounds 명분

| **mojo** | **The bank gives a reason that it comes from Trumplation, but it just lines its own pocket on the grounds that they want to curb household debts.** |

[tip] give a reason 이유다 **it comes from** ~에서 왔다 · 그런 이유다 **it lines own pocket** 주머니에 집어넣다 **on the grounds** 명분으로

| **practice** | The authority is about to look into concerning of lender's burden. |

| **mojo** | **The authority is out to look into market in the fear of expanding the individual debtor' liability.** |

[tip] individual debtor 개인대출자 **liability** 의무 · 책임 · 부채

| **practice** | It is serious that the additional interest is raising movement among banking circles. |

| **mojo** | **It is serious concern that the commercial banks' interest rate are moving up.** |

[tip] commercial bank 은행권 · 시중은행 · 일반상업은행

text

하반기 들어 오름폭이 커지더니 이젠 배(기준금리)와 배꼽(가산금리)의 크기가 별 차이가 없다.

try

[word] 하반기 **the second half of the year · the latter half of the year**
기준금리 **key rate**

text

대출자의 부담이 커진다는 우려가 나오자 금융감독당국이 점검에 나섰다.

try

[word] 금융감독위원회 · 금감원 **the Financial Supervisory Commission**
부담 **burden**

practice

The rising gap has been getting bigger from ~~start of~~ second half of the year, now there is almost no different between Key rate and additional rate.

[Suggestion] from start of → from beginning

mojo

As the ratio of rising has become wide in the second half of this year, now there is barely difference between the key rate and the additional interest rate.

[tip] the ratio of rising 상승비율 **subsidiary expense** 가산금리 · 추가적 비용 **surpass original outlay** 부수비용 **outlay** 지출경비

call rate 콜금리 · 하루 이틀 정도 단기금리

---

practice

Financial Supervisory Commission has come forward to review following worry about bigger burden for ~~lender~~.

[Suggestion] lender 대출해 주는 측 → **debtor** 빌린 측

mojo

The Financial Supervisory Commission has come to examine the situation following the fear that debtors'burden would grow.

[tip] examine 점검 **fear** 우려

following the fear 우려에 뒤이어 · 우려가 나오자

트럼프 아베 회담, 이방카 쿠슈너 펜스 플린 총출동
트럼프타워 68층 자택서 만나

아베 "신뢰할 수 있는 지도자"
트럼프 "친구 관계 시작 영광"

17일 오후 6시 32분 미국 뉴욕 맨해튼 인터콘티넨털호텔 1층.
도널드 트럼프 미 대통령 당선인과의 회담을 마치고 숙소로 돌아온
아베 신조 일본 총리의 표정에선 안도감이 느껴졌다.
아베가 기자들 앞에 나타나 발표한 메시지는 딱 두 가지.
첫째는 "비공식 회담이라 자세한 회담 내용은 밝힐 수 없다"는 것.
아직 대통령 당선인 신분인 트럼프와의 대화를 일일이 밝힐 경우
현 버락 오바마 행정부에 대한 결례라 판단했기 때문이었다.
하지만 "매우 따스한 분위기 속에서 흉금을 터 놓고 대화했고
트럼프는 신뢰할 수 있는 지도자라고 확신했다"고 강조하는 대목에선
아베의 손 제스처가 커졌다.
"서로 괜찮은 시기에 다시 만나서 보다 넓고 깊게 이야기를 나누기로 합의했다"는
말도 덧붙였다.

text	트럼프 아베 회담, 이방카 쿠슈너 펜스 플린 총출동 트럼프타워 68층 자택서 만나
try	

[word] 트럼프 Trump 아베 Abe 이방카 Ivanka 쿠슈너 Kushner 펜스 Pence
플린 Michael T. Flynn 회담 talk

12

Mojo Writing

Trump-Abe talks, in which Ivanka, Kushner, Flynn and Pence all sat together. They met at Trump home, 68th floor of Trump Tower.

Abe said "he is a credible leader," and "friendship relations begin between two countries with pleasure," Trump said.

At the first floor of intercontinental hotel, Manhattan New York. At 6:32 on November 17, Shinzo Abe, the Japanese Prime Minister, exuded a sense of relief right after he came back from talks with the president-elect, Donald Trump, Abe announced on two messages before reporters.
First one was he would not go into details of mutual talks because it was informal talks. It because he is still President-elect and Abe thought it might belittle Obama administration. However, when he intoned hearted dialogue of warmth with Trump and he said he felt confident that Trump is a credible leader, he made a bigger gesture with his hand. "We agreed to meet again to share a broader and deeper talk at a good time" he said

practice

In the talk between Trump and Abe, Ivanka, Kushner, Pence and Flynn ~~were mobilized together~~. They met at Trump's home, 68th of Trump Tower.

[Suggestion] were mobilized together → 동원되었다

mojo

Trump-Abe talks, in which Ivanka, Kushner, PenceandFlynn all sat together. They met at Trump home, 68th floor of Trump Tower.

[tip] all sat together 총출동했다 · 함께 모여 앉았다

text	아베 "신뢰할 수 있는 지도자" 트럼프 "친구 관계 시작 영광"
try	
	[word] 신뢰할 수 있는 **credible** 지도자 **leader** 친구관계 **friendship**

text	17일 오후 6시 32분 미국 뉴욕 맨해튼 인터콘티넨털호텔 1층. 도널드 트럼프 미 대통령 당선인과의 회담을 마치고 숙소로 돌아온 아베 신조 일본 총리의 표정에선 안도감이 느껴졌다.
try	
	[word] 맨해튼 **Manhattan** 인터콘티넨털호텔 **Intercontinental Hotel** 도널드 트럼프 미 대통령 당선인 **Donald Trump, the U.S. President elected** 숙소 **one's lodgings** 아베 신조 일본 총리 **Shinzo Abe, the Japanese Prime Minister**

text	아베가 기자들 앞에 나타나 발표한 메시지는 딱 두 가지. 첫째는 "비공식 회담이라 자세한 회담 내용은 밝힐 수 없다"는 것.
try	
	[word] 기자들 **reports** 발표하다 **announce** 비공식회담 **unofficial conversation**

practice

Abe said "he is a credible leader," while Trump told that "friendship begins a pleasure."

[Suggestion] a pleasure → with pleasure

mojo

Abe said "he is a credible leader," and "friendship relations begin between two countries with pleasure," Trump said.

[tip] with pleasure 영광

---

practice

At the first floor lobbies of Intercontinental Hotel, New York Manhattan the U.S. afternoon 6:32 on November 17, Shinzo Abe, the Japanese Prime Minister, was felted a relief feeling from his face when he returned back at his lodging after finishing talking with the new President-elect, Donald Trump.

[Suggestion] was felted a relief → felt a relief

mojo

At the first floor of Intercontinental Hotel, Manhattan New York. At 6:32 on November 17, Shinzo Abe, the Japanese Prime Minister, exuded a sense of relief right after he came back from talks with the U.S. president-elect, Donald Trump.

[tip] exude 스며나오다 · 발산하다 a sense of relief 안도감

---

practice

What he announced is just two messages. First, "he couldn't reveal precisely about the details due to unofficial conversation" he said.

[Suggestion] revealprecisely about the details → reveal precisely the details

mojo

Abe announced on two messages before reporters. First one was he would not go into details of mutual talks because it was informal talks.

[tip] before reports 기자들 앞에서 not go into details 자세한 내용을 밝히지 않는다 mutual talk 상호회담 informal 비공식

text	아직 대통령 당선인 신분인 트럼프와의 대화를 일일이 밝힐 경우 현 버락 오바마 행정부에 대한 결례라 판단했기 때문이었다.
try	

[word] 아직**yet** 신분 **status** 대화를 일일이 **the each talk**
현 버락 오바마 행정부 **current Barack Obama administration**
결례 · 예절무시 **negligence of etiquette**

text	하지만 "매우 따스한 분위기 속에서 흉금을 터 놓고 대화했고 트럼프는 신뢰할 수 있는 지도자라고 확신했다"고 강조하는 대목에선 아베의 손 제스처가 커졌다.
try	

[word] 따스한 **warm** 흉금 **bosom · heart** 신뢰할 수 있는 지도자 **a credible leader** 제스처 **gesture**

text	"서로 괜찮은 시기에 다시 만나서 보다 넓고 깊게 이야기를 나누기로 합의했다" 는 말도 덧붙였다.
try	

[word] 괜찮은 시기에 **at a good time** 합의하다 **agree** 덧붙이다 **add**

practice	Since Trump is ~~yet~~ a status of president elected, if it revealed the each talk with him, he decided it makes a negligence of etiquette against the Obama administration. **[Suggestion] yet**(부정) → **still**(긍정) · **is not yet**
mojo	**It because he is still President-elect and Abe thought it might belittle Obama administration.** **[tip] still** 아직 · 여전히 **belittle** 과소평가하다 · 얕보다 · 작게하다

practice	But when he stressed ~~part comes~~, as saying "they opened their heart each other and talked in warming air, he confirmed Trump as a credible leader," Abe made a bigger gesture. **[Suggestion] part comes → dialogue**
mojo	**However, when he intoned hearted dialogue of warmth with Trump and he said he felt confident that Trump is a credible leader, he made a bigger gesture with his hand.** **[tip] intone** 특정한 음조로 말하다 · 억양을 붙여서 말하다 **warm hearted dialogue** 마음 따뜻한 대화 **feel confident** 확신하다 **a bigger gesture with his hand** 더 큰 손제스쳐

practice	He added "we ~~will~~ meet again at a good time and ~~agree to deep~~ and various talk. **[Suggestion] will → would agree to deep → agreed deepen**
mojo	**"We agreed to meet again to share a broader and deeper talk at a good time" he added.** **[tip] Agree to meet again** 다시 만나는데 합의하다 **a broader and deeper** 보다 넓고 깊게

“인공호흡기 꽂는 영상 보여주니 연명의료 1명도 선택 안해”
안젤로 볼란데스 하버드대 의대 교수
말기암 환자 고통스런 치료 방지
말로 설명보다 동영상이 효과적

중환자실 대신 가정 완화의료 선택
하와이선 병원사망률 22% 줄어

text	“인공호흡기 꽂는 영상 보여주니 연명의료 1명도 선택 안해” 안젤로 볼란데스 하버드대 의대 교수, 말기암 환자 고통스런 치료 방지, 말로 설명보다 동영상이 효과적
try	

[word] 인공호흡기 **breathing machine** 영상 **video·image·clip·film**

연명의료 **life prolongation** 안젤로 볼란데스 **Angelo Volandes**

하버드 의대교수 **a professor of Harvard medical School**

말기암 **terminal cancer** 치료 **treatment·treat·care** 효과적 **be effective**

13

Life prolongation

Nobody chose to take medical practice for life subsistence when they were shown video of sticking a respirator Angelo Volandes, Harvard Medical School, mentioned that playing video would be more effective than just words to prevent a terminal cancer patient from painful treatment, recommending to choose a home medical relieve medicine.
It led the death rate of cancer in hospital to come down twenty two percent in Hawaii.

practice

"Even one person didn't choose medical care for like prolongation when they ~~were looked~~ the video of using breathing machine." Angelo Volandes who is a professor ~~in~~ Harvard Medical School, said the video was effective than description of words to anti-medical care suffering terminal cancer patients.

[Suggestion] were looked → shown a professor in Harvard Medical School → a professor of Harvard Medical School

mojo

Nobody chose to take medical practice for life subsistence when they were shown video of sticking a respirator Angelo Volandes, Harvard Medical School, mentioned that playing video would be more effective than just words to prevent a terminal cancer patient from painful treatment.

[tip] nobody choose 아무도 선택하지 않는다 **life subsistence** 연명 **sticking a respirator** 인공호흡기 꽂으며 **painful treatment** 고통스런 치료

중환자실 대신 가정 완화의료 선택,
하와이선 병원사망률 22% 줄어

[word] 중환자실 intensive care ward 완화의료 alleviation care

They tended to choose alleviation care at home instead of intensive care ward.The cancer death rate in hospital reduced by 22% in Hawaii.

They chose a home medical relieve medicineinstead of intensive care ward.It led the death rate of cancer in hospital to come down twenty two percent in Hawaii.

[tip] **lead to come down** 줄어드는 것으로 이어지다·연결되다

✎

명동 임대료 세계 8위, 1위는 뉴욕 5번가 중심지

서울 명동이 세계에서 8번째로 임대료가 비싼 상권으로 꼽혔다.
영국의 부동산 컨설팅회사 쿠시먼앤드웨이크필드가 발행한
보고서 2016년 세계의 주요 번화가(Main Streets Across the World 2016)에
따르면 명동의 월평균 임대료는 m^2당 908달러다.
33m^2(10평) 남짓한 작은 매장 하나만 해도 월 임대료가 3,500만 원을 넘는 셈이다.
명동의 평균 임대료는 지난해 같은 조사 때보다 6.3% 상승했다.
순위는 지난해 9위에서 한 계단 올라섰다.
이 보고서는 세계 500여 개 주요 상권의 지난해 3분기부터 올해 2분기까지
1년간 임대료를 조사했다.

text	명동 임대료 세계 8위, 1위는 뉴욕 5번가 중심지
try	[word] 명동 **Myongdong**　임대료 **rent rate** 뉴욕 5번가 **the fifth street of New York City**
text	서울 명동이 세계에서 8번째로 임대료가 비싼 상권으로 꼽혔다.
try	[word] 세계에서 **in the world**　상권 **shopping district**　꼽히다 **be counted**

The house rent in Myongdong is 8th in the world, and the fifth street of New York is the highest.

Myongdong, Seoul has been counted as eighth expensive shopping district in the world. According to the Main Street Across the World released by Cushman & Wakefield, British real estate consult company, the average monthly rental charge is $908 per square meter. For a store of small size about 33 square meters (10 pyong), monthly rent is over 35 million won. It has risen 6.3% compared with same time of last year. Its ranking rose a step up from ninth. The report is showing the surveyed rent of global 500 commercial areas from third quarter last year to second this.

practice	The rent ~~of Myongdong area~~ ranks eighth and the fifth street of New York City is No. one in the world. **[Suggestion] Myongdong area ranks eighth → ranks eighth of Myongdong area**
mojo	**The house rent in Myongdong is 8th in the world, and the fifth street of New York is the highest.** **[tip] the house rent** 임대료
practice	Myongdong in Seoul is counted ~~eighth expensive rent shopping district~~ in the world. **[Suggestion] is counted eighth expensive rent shopping district → is counted for shopping district eighth expensive**
mojo	**Myongdong, Seoul has been counted as eighth expensive shopping district in the world.** **[tip] has been counted** 꼽혔다 **as eighth** 8번째로 According to the report of Main Streets Across the World

text

영국의 부동산 컨설팅회사 쿠시먼앤드웨이크필드가 발행한 보고서 2016년
세계의 주요 번화가에 따르면 명동의 월평균 임대료는 m²당 908달러다.

try

[word] 영국 부동산 컨설팅회사 **British real estate consulting company**
쿠시먼앤드웨이크필드 **Cushman & Wakefield** 2016년 세계의 주요 번화가 **Main
Streets Across the World 2016** 월평균 임대료 **the average of monthly
rental charge**

---

text

33m²(10평) 남짓한 작은 매장 하나만 해도 월 임대료가 3,500만 원을
넘는 셈이다.

try

[word] 작은 매장 하나 **one small store**

---

text

명동의 평균 임대료는 지난해 같은 조사 때보다 6.3% 상승했다.
순위는 지난해 9위에서 한 계단 올라섰다.

try

[word] 지난해 같은 조사 때보다 **same time of last year** 9위에서 한계단 올라서다
ahead on step from ninth

practice	2016 ~~releasing from~~ British real estate consulting company, Cushman & Wakefield, the average of monthly rental charge in Myongdong is \$908 per m^2. **[Suggestion] releasing from British → released by British**
mojo	**According to the Main Street Across the World released by Cushman & Wakefield, British real estate consult company, the average monthly rental charge is \$908 per square meter.** **[tip] \$908 per square meter m^2 908달러**
practice	Even ~~one~~ small store about 33m^2 in the district mean to over 35 million monthly. **[Suggestion] evenone small store → even a small store**
mojo	**For a store of small size about 33 square meters (10 pyong), monthly rent is over 35 million won.** **[tip] for a store of small size about 33 square meters (10 pyong) 33m^2(10평) 남짓한 작은 매장 하나만 해도 is over 35 million won 3,500만 원이 넘는다**
practice	It has risen by 6.3% compare with same time ~~on~~ last year, ranking ahead on step from ninth. **[Suggestion] on last year → of last year**
mojo	**It has risen 6.3% compared with same time of last year. Its ranking rose a step up from ninth.** **[tip] compared with same time of last year 지난해 같은 조사 때와 비교해서 its ranking 순위는**

이 보고서는 세계 500여 개 주요 상권의 지난해 3분기부터 올해 2분기까지 1년간 임대료를 조사했다.

[word] 지난해 3분기부터 **from third quarter of last year**

올해 2분기까지 **to second this year**

The report surveyed the rent of global 500 commercial areas from third quarter last year to second this year.

The report is showing the surveyed rent of global 500 commercial areas from third quarter last year to second this year.

[tip] **global 500 commercial areas** 세계 500여 개 주요 상권

신화속 뱀이 디자인 모티브.. 손목에 똬리 튼 불멸의 예술혼: 불가리

수작업 통해 제작되는 명품 시계
착용감 뛰어나고 관능미도 넘쳐
불가리의 독자적인 기술적 노하우가 탄생시킨
새로운 세르펜티 투보가스(Serpenti Tubogas)가 선보였다.
세르펜티 투보가스는 신비로운 색상의 다이얼을 장착해 매력을 드러낸다.
고대 로마의 전통 우화 속에 등장하는 뱀을 모티브로 한 세르펜티 투보가스는
관능미가 넘치는 작품으로 평가 받는다.
세르펜티는 이태리어로 뱀을 뜻한다.
이름 그대로 옛 그리스와 로마에서 영원한 생명과 지혜,
불멸과 풍요의 상징으로 여겨지던 뱀을 소재로 만든 고급 장신구다.
세르펜티 주얼리 컬렉션은 마치 뱀이 똬리를 틀고 있는 듯한 모습을 통해
뱀의 강한 기운과 역동성을 표현한 것이 특징이다.

text	신화속 뱀이 디자인 모티브.. 손목에 똬리 튼 불멸의 예술혼: 불가리
try	[word] 신화 **myth · mythology** 뱀 **snake** 디자인 모티브 **motive for its design** 손목 **wrist** 똬리 튼 **coiled** 불멸 **immortal** 예술혼 **art spirit** 불가리 **Bvlgari**

15

Mojo Writing

Bvlgari makes the snake in the myth its motive for its design, and its immoral art spirit coiling up on the wrist.

It is a kind of hand-made and fine watch, made for comfort to wear with outflowing sensual aura.

The latest fashion of the Serpenti Tubogas, created by Bvlgari's unique workmanship, has come into a display. The dial inlaid to the mystic color tone is adding charms to the watch.

The Serpentine Tubogas representing the snake appearing in the traditional Rome fables is appreciated to be works of overflowing beauty.

The Serpenti means snake in Italian. The snake meant to be a source of an eternal life, wisdom and affluence, is embodied in the high-end jewelry. The collection of the Serpenti is characterized of a dynamic and strong power out of the figure, like as it twists its body.

practice	Bvlgari brings snake in myth into motive for its design, ~~making~~ it coiled round wrist as immortal art spirit. **[Suggestion] makingit coiled → getting it coil**
mojo	**Bvlgari makes the snake in the myth its motive for its design, and its immoral art spirit coiling up on the wrist.** **[tip] Bvlgari makes the snake in the myth** 불가리는 신화속 뱀을 만들었다 **its immoral art spirit coiling up** 똬리 튼 불멸의 예술혼

| **text** | 수작업 통해 제작되는 명품 시계, 착용감 뛰어나고 관능미도 넘쳐 |
| **try** | |

[word] 수작업 hand-made 명품 시계 **the masterpiece watch** 착용감 **comfort**
관능미 **voluptuous beauty**

| **text** | 불가리의 독자적인 기술적 노하우가 탄생시킨 새로운 세르펜티 투보가스가 선보였다. |
| **try** | |

[word] 독자적인 기술 **unique workmanship** 세르펜티 투보가스 **Serpenti Tubogas**

| **text** | 세르펜티 투보가스는 신비로운 색상의 다이얼을 장착해 매력을 드러낸다. |
| **try** | |

[word] 신비로운 색상 **mystic color**

practice Not only has it super fitting on wrist, but also ~~outflows voluptuous beauty~~.

[Suggestion] outflows voluptuous beauty → voluptuous beauty outflows 관능적인 아름다움이 넘치다

mojo The latest fashion of the Serpenti Tubogas, created by Bvlgari's unique workmanship, has come into a display.

[tip] the latest fashion 새로운 노하우 · 방식 **has come into a display** 선보였다

---

practice It is kind of the masterpiece watch producing with manual labor.

mojo It is a kind of hand-made and fine watch, made for comfort to wear with outflowing sensual aura.

[tip] and fine watch, made → and fine watch, (which was) made
fine watch 명품 시계 **for comfort to wear** 착용감 뛰어나고
outflowing sensual aura 관능미 넘쳐

---

practice The Serpenti Tubogas created by BVLGARI's unique technological skill, shows its new ~~lines~~.

[Suggestion] lines → charm

mojo The dial inlaid to the mystic color tone is adding charms to the watch.

[tip] the dial inlaid 다이얼을 장착해 **the mystic color tone** 신비로운 색상 톤 **add charms to the watch** 시계에 매력을 더하다

text

고대 로마의 전통 우화 속에 등장하는 뱀을 모티브로 한 세르펜티 투보가스는 관능미가 넘치는 작품으로 평가 받는다.

try

[word] 고대 로마 **ancient Rome** 전통 우화 **traditional fables** 평가 **evaluate**

text

세르펜티는 이태리어로 뱀을 뜻한다.

try

[word] 이태리어 **Italian** 뜻하다 **mean**

text

이름 그대로 옛 그리스와 로마에서 영원한 생명과 지혜, 불멸과 풍요의 상징으로 여겨지던 뱀을 소재로 만든 고급 장신구다.

try

[word] 이름 그대로 **as its name** 영원한 생명과 지혜 **eternal life and wisdom**
고급 장신구 **luxury accessory**

practice

The pieces are evaluated ~~arts~~ of overflowing voluptuous beauty as a motivated snake appearing a traditional allegory in ancient Rome. The Serpenti Tubogas reveals charm itself equipping dials of mystery colors.

[Suggestion] evaluated arts → evaluated to be as arts of

mojo

The Serpentine Tubogas representing the snake appearing in the traditional Rome fables is appreciated to be works of overflowing beauty.

[tip] **Representing the snake** 뱀을 나타내는 · 동기 · 모티브 **is appreciated to** 평가 받다 **outflowing beauty** 관능미가 넘치는

---

practice

Serpenti means a snake in Italic.

mojo

The Serpenti means snake in Italian.

---

practice

As its name, the luxury accessories made with materials of snake which deemed a symbol of eternal life, wisdom, immortal and affluent in ancient Greece and Rome.

mojo

The snake meant to be a source of an eternal life, wisdom, and affluence, is embodied in the high-end jewelry.

[tip] **a source** 소재 **beembodied** 형태가 부여되다 · 구현되다 **the high-end jewelry** 최고급 장신구

세르펜티 주얼리 컬렉션은 마치 뱀이 똬리를 틀고 있는 듯한 모습을 통해 뱀의 강한 기운과 역동성을 표현한 것이 특징이다.

[word] 컬렉션 **collection** 강한 기운과 역동성 **dynamic and strong power**

practice

The collection ~~featured~~ expressions of snake's dynamic and strong power, like as it shapes a twisting body.

[Suggestion] featured → is feature to be

mojo

The collection of the Serpenti is characterized of a dynamic and strong power out of the figure, like as it twists its body.

[tip] is characterized 특징이다 **as it twists its body** 마치 그것이 몸을 비틀고 있는 것처럼

'트럼트 반대' 깃발 든 메르켈 "개방이 고립보다 안전 보장"

개방과 포용, 그리고 자유무역.

앙겔라 메르켈 독일 총리가 23일 연방하원 정책토론회 연설에서 내보인 메시지다.

총리 4선 도전을 선언한 그로선 첫 주요 연설이었다.

그는 이날 도널드 트럼프 미국 대통령 당선인을 거명하지 않았다.

그러나 언론들은 "트럼프와 대조되는 입장을 내보이며 선거운동을 시작했다"고
분석했다.

그는 테러 이민 세계화에 대한 일반인들의 우려에 공감했다.

그리곤 이민정책부터 복지까지 안전과 자유를 지키겠다고 다짐했다.

"우리는 세계화의 모습을 만들어 가는데 있어서 다자주의를 지지해야 한다"며
"나도 그러겠다"고 말했다.

text	'트럼트 반대' 깃발 든 메르켈 "개방이 고립보다 안전 보장"
try	

[word] 트럼프 반대 **anti-Trump** 메르켈 **Angela Merkel** 개방 **open**
고립 **isolation** 안정 **stable** 보장 **guarantee**

16

Mojo Writing

Angela Merkel holding a banner standing up to Trump, insists that an open policy guarantees security over isolation.

Openness, tolerance and free trade, are message which Angela Merkel, German Chancellor, delivered of her speech at the discussion forum on her policy on November 23. It was her main speech, in which she announced her fourth race for Prime Minister Position. On the day she didn't name Donald Trump but media and journalism analyzed that she launched her campaign, showing her position in contrast to Trump. She shared the fears of public about globalized migration from terror.

She has vowed to keep security and freedom in order from immigration policy to welfare. "We have to advocate pluralism shaping the globalizations.So will do I." She said.

practice	Angela Merkel holding with a flag of anti-Trump insisted "the opening policy guarantees security ~~than~~ the closing one." **[Suggestion] than → over the closing one · isolation**
mojo	**Angela Merkel holding a banner standing up to Trump, insists that an open policy guarantees security over isolation.** **[tip] holding a banner** 깃발 든 **standing up** 트럼프에게 맞서는 **insist** 주장하다 **open policy** 개방정책

<table>
<tr><td>text</td><td>개방과 포용, 그리고 자유무역.앙겔라 메르켈 독일 총리가 23일 연방하원 정책토론회 연설에서 내보인 메시지다.</td></tr>
<tr><td>try</td><td></td></tr>
<tr><td></td><td>[word] 포용 embracement 자유무역 free trade 총리 Chancellor of German
독일 연방하원 Bundestag (Federal)</td></tr>
<tr><td>text</td><td>총리 4선 도전을 선언한 그로선 첫 주요 연설이었다.</td></tr>
<tr><td>try</td><td></td></tr>
<tr><td></td><td>[word] 4선 도전 fourth challenge 연설 speech</td></tr>
<tr><td>text</td><td>그는 이날 도널드 트럼프 미국 대통령 당선인을 거명하지 않았다. 그러나 언론들은 "트럼프와 대조되는 입장을 내보이며 선거운동을 시작했다"고 분석했다.</td></tr>
<tr><td>try</td><td></td></tr>
<tr><td></td><td>[word] 거명하다 do the name 언론 media 대조 contrast
선거운동 election campaign</td></tr>
</table>

practice

Openness, ~~embracement~~ and free trade. It was a message that Angela Merckel, current Chancellor of German, brought speech of policy discussion in Bundestag on November 23.

[Suggestion] embracement 포옹 → **tolerance** 포용

mojo

Openness, tolerance and free trade, are message which Angela Merkel, German Chancellor, delivered of her speech at the discussion forum on her policy on November 23.

[tip] tolerance 관용 · 포용력 · 받아들이다 **delivered of her speech** 그녀의 연설에서 내보인 **at the discussion forum** 토론회에서

practice

As she is throwing fourth ~~challenge of~~ the chancellor position, it was first important speech.

[Suggestion] challenge of → **race for**

mojo

It was her main speech, in which she announced her fourth race for Prime Minister Position.

[tip] main speech 주요 연설 **her fourth race** 4선 도전

for Prime Minister Position 총리직책에

practice

She didn't ~~call the name~~ of the U.S. president-elect Donald Trump, but medias analyzed she has started campaign for showing contrast position ~~against~~ Trump.

[Suggestion] didn't call the name 욕하다 → **didn't the name** 거명하지 않았다 **contrastposition against Trump** → **contrast position Trump**

mojo

On the day she didn't name Donald Trump but media and journalism analyzed that she launched her campaign, showing her position in contrast to Trump.

[tip] launch 시작하다 **in contrast to** 대조되는

text

그는 테러 이민 세계화에 대한 일반인들의 우려에 공감했다. 그리곤 이민정책 부터 복지까지 안전과 자유를 지키겠다고 다짐했다.

try

[word] 테러 이민 세계화 **global terror migration** 공감 **empathy·sympathy** 복지 **welfare** 자유 **freedom**

---

text

"우리는 세계화의 모습을 만들어 가는데 있어서 다자주의를 지지해야 한다"며 "나도 그러겠다"고 말했다.

try

[word] 다자주의 **multilateralism** 지지 **advocate**

practice

She has sympathized with people concerning about global terror migration and made ~~a promise keeping~~ security and freedom from immigration policy to welfare.

[Suggestion] a promise keeping → to keep a promise

mojo

She shared the fears of public about globalized migration from terror.She has vowed to keep security and freedom in order from immigration policy to welfare.

[tip] **share** 공감하다 **the fears of public** 일반인의 두려움 **vow** 다짐하다

from immigration policy to welfare 이민 정책에서부터 복지까지

---

practice

She said "we have to advocate multilateralism when globalization is making its shape, and so do I."

mojo

"We have to advocate pluralism shaping the globalizations. So will do I." She said.

[tip] **advocate pluralism** 다자주의 옹호 **so will do I** 나도 그러겠다

✏️

닮은 점

1997월 11월 vs 2016년 11월… 닮은 점이 신경 쓰인다
리더십 사라지고 IMF는 부채 경고
제조업 가동률 뚝뚝, 관료 팔짱만
한국 경제 퍼펙트 스톰 우려 커져
국가 신용 높고 외환보유액은 넉넉
"성장 잠재력 높일 특단대책 필요"

"정부는 최근 겪고 있는 금융 외환시장에서의 어려움을 극복하기 위해
국제통화기금 (IMF)에 자금 지원을 요청하기로 결정했습니다."
19년 전인 1997년 11월 21일 오후,
당시 임창열 부총리 겸 재정경제원장관이 발표문을 읽었다.
다소 잠긴 목소리였다.
결국 한국이 IMF에 구제금융을 신청했다는 뉴스는
이렇게 전 세계로 타전됐다.
2016년의 11월 지금은 1997년 외환위기의 악몽에서 얼마나 자유로운가.
불행히도 꼭 그렇지는 않다.
제조업 가동률은 70%대로 떨어졌고
구조조정에 내몰린 기업들은 불확실성의 바다에서 허우적댄다.
대통령 지지율은 5%로 추락했고
최순실 스캔들로 정치권의 공방 속에 리더십이 실종됐다.
조타수를 잃은 공무원들은 일손을 놓았다.

text	1997월 11월 vs 2016년 11월… 닮은 점이 신경 쓰인다
try	
	[word] 닮은 점 the resemblance 신경 nerve·care

17

Mojo Writing

The resemblance

We start to get on our nerves about the resemblance between the November 1997 and November 2016: Leadership has gone out of sight and IMF warned about the debt of Korean economy, the rate of operation of manufacturing is falling down, the bureaucracy is only arms crossing, the perfect storming to Korean economy has assumed very serious concern. That's all true, but its sovereign rate is still high, and it's foreign exchange reserve is enough as yet. "The country needs to take extraordinary measures to enhance potential for growth," "our government has decided to apply for bailout fund to IMF to overcome foreign exchange crisis." The then deputy Prime Minister, Financial Economic Minister, read the announcement in the afternoon of November 1997, back to 19 years. He read it in hoarse voice. The news was wired all over the world immediately.

How much free is now the month of November 2016 out of the nightmare of the financial crisis? Unfortunately, it is not quite so. New dimension of concern has been added that the operation rate of manufacture has fallen down 70% and businesses sidelined by restructuring are struggling to survive on the sea of uncertainty. President approval rate has sunk down to 5%. The readership has disappeared amid political battle over Chwey Sunsil's scandal. The public service has almost stopped working losing the helmsman.

practice	The imaginary of ~~resembled~~ November between 1997 and 2016 makes us fear.
	[Suggestion] resembled 닮은 → resemblance 닮은점 · 유사점
mojo	**We start to get on our nerves about the resemblance between the November 1997 and November 2016:**
	[tip] **to get on our nerves** 신경 쓰인다

text	리더십 사라지고 IMF는 부채 경고 제조업 가동률 뚝뚝, 관료 팔짱만 한국 경제 퍼펙트 스톰 우려 커져 국가 신용 높고 외환보유액은 넉넉
try	
	[word] 국제통화기금 International Monetary Fund (IMF) 부채 debt 제조업 가동률 the operation rate of manufacture 관료 bureaucrat 퍼펙트 스톰 perfect storm 국가 신용 sovereign rate 외환보유액 foreign exchange reserve
text	"성장 잠재력 높일 특단대책 필요"
try	[word] 성장 잠재력 growing potential
text	"정부는 최근 겪고 있는 금융 외환시장에서의 어려움을 극복하기 위해 국제통화기금 (IMF)에 자금 지원을 요청하기로 결정했습니다."
try	[word] 정부 government 외환시장 foreign exchange market 극복 overcome

| **practice** | Korean economy has taken debt warning by IMF, going out of leadership, falling down movability of manufactures, and increasingly raised concern about perfect storming to it, when bureaucrats are crossing their arms here. Although Korean sovereign credit rating still high and the holding of foreign exchange has enough.

[Suggestion] taken debt warning → taken warning of debt |

mojo

Leadership has gone out of sight and IMF warned about the debt of Korean economy, the rate of operation of manufacturing is falling down, the bureaucracy is only arms crossing, the perfect storming to Korean economy has assumed very serious concern. That's all true, but its sovereign rate is still high, and it's foreign exchange reserve is enough as yet.

---

practice

"The country must ~~ensure~~ to extraordinary measures to leverage up of potential growing."

[Suggestion] ensure → need

mojo

"The country needs to take extraordinary measures to enhance potential for growth."

---

practice

"Government has decided to ask for supporting funds at IMF to overcome ~~difficulties suffering in~~ foreign exchange market."

[Suggestion] to overcome foreign exchange market

mojo

"Our government has decided to apply for bailout fund to IMF to overcome foreign exchange crisis."

[tip] has decided to apply for bailout fund 구제금융을 요청하기로 결정했다

19년 전인 1997년 11월 21일 오후, 당시 임창열 부총리 겸 재정경제원장관
이 발표문을 읽었다. 다소 잠긴 목소리였다.

[word] 부총리 겸 재정경제원장관 **deputy Prime Minister and Ministry of financial affairs** 다소 잠긴 목소리 **hoarse voice**

결국 한국이 IMF에 구제금융을 신청했다는 뉴스는 이렇게 전 세계로 타전됐다.

[word] 결국 **finally** 구제금융 **supporting fund** 신청 **apply**

2016년의 11월 지금은 1997년 외환위기의 악몽에서 얼마나 자유로운가.
불행히도 꼭 그렇지는 않다.

[word] 외환위기 **financial crisis** 악몽 **nightmare** 얼마나 **how much**
불행히도 **unfortunately**

In the afternoon on November 21, 1997, back to 19 years, then Yim Chungrol who was deputy Prime Minister and Ministry of financial affairs revealed a statement with hoarse voice.
[Suggestion] Chungrol who → Chungrol, who astatement with hoarse voice → a statement in hoarse voice

The then deputy Prime Minister, Financial Economic Minister, read the announcement in the afternoon of November 1997, back to 19 years.He read it in hoarse voice.
[tip] the announcement 발표문 back to 19 years 19년 전 당시

Finally, the news for Korea to apply supporting fund at IMF had sent to all of the world this way.
[Suggestion] supporting fund at IMF had sent toall of the world → bailout fund to IMF had been sent toall the world

The news was wired all over the world immediately.
[tip] was wired 타전됐다 immediately 즉시

How much free now, the month of November, 2016 from the nightmare of financial crisis? Unfortunately, it isn't that surely. How much free now, November 2016 out of the nightmare

How much free is now the month of November 2016 out of the nightmare of the financial crisis? Unfortunately, it is not quite so.
[tip] not quite so 꼭 그렇지 않다

제조업 가동률은 70%대로 떨어졌고 구조조정에 내몰린 기업들은 불확실성의 바다에서 허우적댄다.

try

[word] 제조업 가동률 **the operation rate of manufacture**
불확실성 **uncertainty**

text

대통령 지지율은 5%로 추락했고 최순실 스캔들로 정치권의 공방 속에 리더십이 실종됐다. 조타수를 잃은 공무원들은 일손을 놓았다.

try

[word] 대통령 지지율 **president approval rate** 최순실 스캔들 **Chwey Sunsil scandal** 정치권의 공방 **political battle** 리더십 **leadership** 공무원 **the public service·the civil service** 조타수 **helmsman**

practice

Manufactural movability fell ~~down 70% level~~, and businesses are driven out restructuring and struggling in the sea of uncertainty.

[Suggestion] down 70% level → down to 70% level

mojo

New dimension of concern has been added that the operation rate of manufacture has fallen down 70% and businesses sidelined by restructuring are struggling to survive on the sea of uncertainty.

[tip] new dimension 새로운 차원 **sidelined** 내몰리다 **struggling to survive** 살기 위해 허우적대다

---

practice

Approval rate for President has sunk ~~at~~ 5%, and the leadership ~~has lost~~ in political controversy by Chwey Sunsil scandal. The civil services have lost their helm and then let their working hands go.

[Suggestion] has sunk 5%, and the leadership has been lost

mojo

President approval rate has sunk down to 5%. The readership has disappeared amid political battle over Chwey Sunsil's scandal. The public service has almost stopped working losing the helmsman.

[tip] sink down 감소하다 · 추락하다 **disappear** 사라지다 · 실종되다 **almost stopped working** 거의 일손을 놓았다

신 개념 웨어러블 백팩 '아르켄'

조끼처럼 편안하게 입고 벗는다: 쌤소나이트 레드

감각적이고 세련된 캐주얼 가방 브랜드인 쌤소나이트 레드가
조끼처럼 입고 벗는 신개념의 웨어러블 백팩을 선보였다.
쌤소나이트 레드가 본격 겨울철을 앞두고 두터운 옷차림에 구애 받지 않으면서
편안하게 착용할 수 있는 울트라슬림 조끼형 백팩 아르캔(Arken)을 출시했다.
특수 원단은 미국 항공우주국 나사(NASA)에서
우주복 제작을 목적으로 만든 온도조절 신소재로서,
주로 아웃도어 제품이나 기능성 정장 등 의류제품에 사용되고 있다.
아르캔은 더운 여름엔 쾌적한 사용감을 제공하고,
추운 겨울철에는 아우터 안쪽에 착용이 가능하다.
이런 경우 옷을 덧입은 것과 같은 방한효과를 발휘한다.

text	신 개념 웨어러블 백팩 '아르켄' 조끼처럼 편안하게 입고 벗는다: 쌤소나이트 레드
try	
	[word] 신 개념 **new concept** 웨어러블 **wearable** 백팩 **backpack**
text	감각적이고 세련된 캐주얼 가방 브랜드인 쌤소나이트 레드가 조끼처럼 입고 벗는 신개념의 웨어러블 백팩을 선보였다.
try	
	[word] 감각적이고 세련된 **elegance** 입고 벗는 **put on and off**

18

Mojo Writing

'Arken' wearable backpack of a new concept is easy to wear or take it off like a vest.

Somsonite Red, sensual and sophisticated casual bag brand, has introduced the new conceptual wearable backpack. It has released wearable ultra-slim vest-type backpack, Arken, without getting hung up on some thick clothes for winter season.

Its special fabrics designed to make NASA spacesuit, is a newly developed material for purpose of temperature adjustment, which is mainly used in outdoor's wear, working suit and clothes. The 'Arken' gives pleasant feeling in summer, and allows it to be inside wear with outer, giving an effect on keeping out cold same way as wearing several layers.

practice	'Arken,' a wearable backpack is a new concept of bag. It is ~~possible~~ to wear like vest, Samsonite Red. **[Suggestion] it is possible to wear → it is easy to wear**
mojo	**'Arken' wearable backpack of a new concept is easy to wear or take it off like a vest.** **[tip] easy to wear or take it off** 편안하게 입고 벗는다

practice	Samsonite Red, ~~sensuous~~ and elegance bag brand, shows a wearable backpack of a new idea of putting on-off like vest. **[Suggestion] sensuous** 예민한 → **sensual** 육체적 감각이 있는 · 관능적인
mojo	**Somsonite Red, sensual and sophisticated casual bag brand, has introduced the new conceptual wearable backpack.** **[tip] sensual and sophisticated** 감각적이고 세련된 **introduced** 선보이다 · 소개하다

text

쌤소나이트 레드가 본격 겨울철을 앞두고 두터운 옷차림에 구애 받지 않으면서 편안하게 착용할 수 있는 울트라슬림 조끼형 백팩 아르캔(Arken)을 출시했다.

try

[word] 두터운 옷차림 **thick clothing** 구애 받다 **disrupt** 울트라슬림 조끼형 **ultra-slim vest-type** 출시하다 **roll out**

text

특수 원단은 미국 항공우주국 나사에서 우주복 제작을 목적으로 만든 온도조절 신소재로서, 주로 아웃도어 제품이나 기능성 정장 등 의류제품에 사용되고 있다.

try

[word] 특수 원단 **special fabrics** 미국 항공우주국 나사 **NASA** 우주복 **spacesuit** 목적으로 **aimed to** 온도조절 **temperature adjustment** 신소재 **new material**

text

아르캔은 더운 여름엔 쾌적한 사용감을 제공하고, 추운 겨울철에는 아우터 안쪽에 착용이 가능하다. 이런 경우 옷을 덧입은 것과 같은 방한효과를 발휘한다.

try

[word] 쾌적한 **comfortable** 착용 **wear** 덧입다 **layers of clothing**

practice

The brand rolled out Arken that is wearable comport ultra-slim vest-type backpack undisrupted ~~any~~ thick clothing for coming winter season.

[Suggestion] any → some

mojo

It has released wearable ultra-slim vest-type backpack, Arken, without getting hung upon some thick clothes for winter season.

[tip] **release** 출시하다 **hung up on** 구애 받다

---

practice

The special fabrics aimed to make a spacesuit in NASA, is new material for being able to adjust at any temperature, mainly ~~using~~ garment for outdoor and functional suit.

[Suggestion] using → being used to make

mojo

Its special fabrics designed to make NASA spacesuit, is a newly developed material for purpose of temperature adjustment, which is mainly used in outdoor's wear, working suit and clothes.

[tip] **designe to** 계획되다 **a newly developed material** 신소재 · 새로 개발된 소재 **for purpose of temperature adjustment** 온도조절이 가능한

---

practice

Arken gives pleasant ~~fitting sense~~ in summer, and can be wear as inner inside jacket in winter working effect as protecting cold layered coat.

[Suggestion] fitting sense → feeling

mojo

The 'Arken' gives pleasant feeling in summer, and allows it to be inside wear with outer, giving an effect on keeping out cold same way as wearing several layers.

[tip] **keeping out cold same way as** 같은 방법으로 방한효과를 유지하는

베를린·멜버른의 별난 커피 향, 서울 거리에 솔솔~

요즘 유럽과 호주 등에서 이름난 유명 로컬 커피 로스터드 브랜드가
서울에 속속 상륙하고 있다.
독일 베를린의 보난자 커피, 호주 멜버른의 듁스 커피,
영국 런던의 스퀘어마일 커피가 대표적이다.
커피 애호가라면 여행 가서 꼭 들른다는,
현지의 스페셜티 커피 트렌드를 이끄는 브랜드들이다.
지난 1일 서울 한남동에 문을 연 mlt카페.
의류 잡화 편집 매장인 모어댄레스 한쪽에 숍인숍(shop in shop) 형태로
들어온 작은 카페지만, 가오픈 기간부터 사람이 몰렸다.
독일 베를린의 '보난자 커피'를 맛볼 수 있다는 입소문이 나면서부터다.

text	베를린·멜버른의 별난 커피 향, 서울 거리에 솔솔~
try	[word] 베를린 **Belin** 멜버른 **Melbourne** 솔솔(떠다닌다) **floating in the air**

19

Mojo Writing

The aroma smell of Berlin or Melbourne wafts up through Seoul Streets.

Of late some popular local coffees of the Europe and Australia, boasted brands, are arriving one after another in Seoul. German Berlin 'Bonanza' coffee, Austrailian Melbourne 'Dukes' coffee and England London 'Squaremile' coffee are typical of them. They are brands ushering in the trends of the local specialty coffees, and coffee lovers will not fail to stop in to taste the coffee on their travel. The mlt café opened on first day of last month is small café in the form of shop in shop of Moretheless for wear and goods. People were rushing in since its opening in working. It is since a buzz of excited chatter of the coffee taste Berlin coffee 'Bonanza.

practice	In the street of Seoul, some unusual coffee ~~smells~~ of Belin or Melbourne are floating in the air. **[Suggestion] coffee smells → coffee smell**
mojo	**The coffee aroma smell of Berlin or Melbourne wafts up through Seoul streets.** **[tip] coffee aroma** 커피향 **waft up** 떠돌다 · 솔솔불다

<table>
<tr><td>text</td><td>요즘 유럽과 호주 등에서 이름난 유명 로컬 커피 로스터드 브랜드가 서울에 속속 상륙하고 있다. 독일 베를린의 보난자 커피, 호주 멜버른의 둑스 커피, 영국 런던의 스퀘어마일 커피가 대표적이다.</td></tr>
<tr><td>try</td><td></td></tr>
</table>

[word] 이름난 **popular**　로스터드 브랜드 **roasted brand**　속속 **one after another**　상륙하다 **land**　보난자 커피 **Bonanza coffee**　둑스 커피 **Dukes coffee**　스퀘어마일 커피 **Squaremile coffee**

<table>
<tr><td>text</td><td>커피 애호가라면 여행 가서 꼭 들른다는, 현지의 스페셜티 커피 트렌드를 이끄는 브랜드들이다.</td></tr>
<tr><td>try</td><td></td></tr>
</table>

[word] 커피 애호가 **coffee lover**　꼭 들르는 곳 **stop by hotspot**

<table>
<tr><td>text</td><td>지난 1일 서울 한남동에 문을 연 mlt카페. 의류 · 잡화 편집 매장인 모어댄레스 한쪽에 숍인숍 형태로 들어온 작은 카페지만, 가오픈 기간부터 사람이 몰렸다.</td></tr>
<tr><td>try</td><td></td></tr>
</table>

[word] 모어댄레스 **more than less**　한쪽에 **corner**　숍인숍 **shop in shop**

practice

Some popular roasted coffee brands ~~in~~ Europe and Australia
have started to land in Seoul one after another recently,
including famous for roasting coffee locally such as leading
Bonanza coffee in Belin, German, Dukes coffee in Melbourne,
Australia and Squaremile coffee in London, the U.K.

[Suggestion] inEurope → of Europe

mojo

**Of late some popular local coffees of the Europe and
Australia, boasted brands, are arriving one after another
in Seoul. German Berlin 'Bonanza' coffee, Austrailian
Melbourne 'Dukes' coffee and England London 'Squaremile'
coffee are typical of them.**

[tip] of late 최근 · 요즘 **boasted** 뽐내는 · 자랑하는

---

practice

Saying without ~~fail~~ stopping by hotspot in travel, if you are a coffee
lover, those brands are driving trend specialty coffee in each local

[Suggestion] fail → failure of

mojo

**They are brands ushering in the trends of the local specialty
coffees, and coffee lovers will not fail to stop in to taste the
coffee on their travel.**

[tip] usher 안내하다 · 이끌다

---

practice

The mlt café was opened in Hannamdong, Seoul last on first
day of November. The café is small and a type of shop in shop
where is ~~in~~ a side corner of Morethanless, a kind of shop
consist with clothes, general goods store, but people flocked
in it from arranging period.

[Suggestion] where is in a side corner → where is at a side corner

mojo

**The mlt café opened on first day of last month is small café
in the form of shop in shop of Moretheless for wear and
goods. People were rushing in since its opening in working.**

[tip] The form of shop in shop 숍인숍 형태 **be rush in** 몰리다

독일 베를린의 '보난자 커피'를 맛볼 수 있다는 입소문이 나면서부터다.

[word] 커피를 맛보다 **taste coffee**

~~Because~~ it has gone viral through mouth that it could taste Bonanza coffee of Belin at the spot.

[Suggestion] because it has gone → it has gone

It is since a buzz of excited chatter of the coffee taste Berlin coffee 'Bonanza.'

[tip] a buzz of excited chatter 입소문 나다

전문가가 꼽은 최고 '피노누아'(마르케스)는 칠레산

"신은 카베르네 쇼비뇽(이하 카쇼)을 만들었고,
악마는 피노누아 (Pinot Noir)를 만들었다."
와인 애호가들 사이에 격언처럼 전해지는 말이다.
피노누아(포도 품종) 와인에 한번 빠지면 헤어나올 수 없고,
와인에 관심을 가지면 궁극적으로 피노누아에 빠지게 된다는 뜻이기도 하다.
피노누아는 카베르네 쇼비뇽에 비해 껍질이 얇고 포도알이 촘촘한데,
기후와 환경에 민감해 재배가 어렵다.
프랑스 부르고뉴 지방에서 재배되는 대표적인 품종이다.
와인컨슈머 리포트 시즌3 첫회 주제는 이 피노누아 와인이다.
카쇼보다 맛이 연하면서도 고급스럽다.

text	전문가가 꼽은 최고 '피노누아'(마르케스)는 칠레산
try	
	[word] 전문가 **expert** 꼽은 **count** 피노누아 **Pinot Noir** 프랑스 부르고뉴 지방 적포도주 품종
text	"신은 카베르네 쇼비뇽(이하 카쇼)을 만들었고, 악마는 피노누아를 만들었다." 와인 애호가들 사이에 격언처럼 전해지는 말이다.
try	
	[word] 카베르네 쇼비뇽 **Cabernet Sauvignon**(적포도주 품종) 악마 **devil** 격언 **maxim**

20

The guru pointed out Chilean wines as the best Pinot Noir.

Among the wine lovers, there is an old proverb that says "The God creates Cabernet Sauvignon and the devil makes Pinot Noir." It implies that when being indulged in the Pinot Noir, grape breeding, it is almost impossible to get out of it, and once having interest in the wine, it eventually leads to addicting to Pinot Noir. It has thinner peel, compared with Cabernet Sauvignon, and in the bunch, the grape is close grained. It is too sensitive to its environment and climate to cultivate it. It is cultivar typical growing in the Bourgogne, France.
The first theme of season 3, consumer report is the Pinot Noir wine. It is high quality and tastes softcompare with Cabernet Sauvignon.

practice	What many experts counted at top Pinot Noir (Marques) is made inChile.
mojo	**The guru pointed out Chilean wines as the best Pinot Noir.** [tip] **guru** 전문가 **point out** 가리키다 · 지적하다 · 밝히다
practice	"God creates Cabernet Sauvignon, and devil makes Pinot Noir." It is saying like maxim among wine lovers.
mojo	**Among the wine lovers, there is an old proverb that says"The God creates Cabernet Sauvignon and the devil makes Pinot Noir."** [tip] **old proverb that says** 이런 격언

text	피노누아(포도 품종) 와인에 한번 빠지면 헤어나올 수 없고, 와인에 관심을 가지면 궁극적으로 피노누아에 빠지게 된다는 뜻이기도 하다.
try	
	[word] 빠지다 · 탐닉하다 **indulge**　헤어나오다 **get out of**　궁극적 **finally** 중독 **addict**

text	카베르네 쇼비뇽에 비해 껍질이 얇고 포도알이 촘촘한데, 기후와 환경에 민감해 재배가 어렵다.
try	
	[word] 껍질 **peel**　밀집 **dense**　포도 송이 **bunch of grapes**　재배 **cultivation**

text	프랑스 부르고뉴 지방에서 재배되는 대표적인 품종이다.
try	
	[word] 지방 **region**　전형적인 · 특유한 **typical**

text	와인컨슈머 리포트 시즌3 첫회 주제는 이 피노누아 와인이다.
try	
	[word] 컨슈머 리포트 · 소비자 보고 **consumer report**

practice

If you indulge in its taste, nobody get out of the wine of Pinot Noir, a kind of grapes, and once having interest in wines, finally it leads to addicting to Pinot Noir.

mojo

[tip] **imply** 뜻이 있다 **itis almost impossible** 거의 불가능하다

grape breeding 포도 품종 **once** 일단 **lead to** ~로 이어지다

---

practice

Pinot Noir has thin peel and denser bunch of grapes than Cabernet Sauvignon, and is hard to ~~cultivation~~ because of sensitivity of climate or growing condition.

[Suggestion] **is hard to cultivation → is hard to cultivate**

mojo

It has thinner peel, compared with Cabernet Sauvignon, and in the bunch, the grape is close grained. It is too sensitive to its environment and climate to cultivate it.

[tip] **compare with** 비교 **compare to** 비유

is close grained 알갱이가 촘촘하다 **too ~ to** 너무 ~하기 어렵다

---

practice

It is a typical variety from the region of Bourgogne, France.

It is a cultivar of typical growing in the Bourgogne, France.

[tip] **cultivar** 품종

---

practice

The first ~~round's~~ theme is wine of Pinot Noir, according to Wine consumer report in third season.

[Suggestion] **the first round's theme → the first theme**

mojo

The first theme of season 3, consumer report is the Pinot Noir wine.

[tip] **is the Pinot Noir wine** 소비자 보고는 피노누아 와인이다

카쇼보다 맛이 연하면서도 고급스럽다.

[**word**] 연하다 **soft**

practice

It tastes soft and quality is ~~high~~ compare with Cabernet Sauvignon.

[Suggestion] high → higher

mojo

It is high quality and tastes soft compare with Cabernet Sauvignon

[tip] high quality and tastes soft 고급스럽고 연한 맛

메시아는 기대하지 말라

치밀하고 꼼꼼한 특수부 검사가 있었다.
구수한 인간미에 균형 감각도 갖춰
어떤 일을 맡아도 소임을 다할 것 같았다.
정치 권력에 줄대기가 잦은 검찰을 저런 이들이 이끌면
기대를 걸어도 되지 않을까 생각하곤 했다.
하지만 박근혜 정부 출범 이후 그는 대형 로펌의 변호사로 옮겼다.
여전히 작업에 열심이고 높은 연봉을 받지만
대한민국 검찰에 그와 같은 이들이 왜 남아 있을 수 없었는지 안타깝다.
박대통령과 측근들에 대한 수사가 한창인 요즘,
검찰이 추상 같은 잣대로 무장했더라면
이 지경이 됐을까 싶어 아쉬움이 더 크다.

text	메시아는 기대하지 말라
try	
	[word] 메시아 **messiah** 기대하다 **expect**

text	치밀하고 꼼꼼한 특수부 검사가 있었다.
try	
	[word] 치밀 · 정교 **elaborate** 꼼꼼하다 **meticulous** 특수부 검사 **special prosecutor**

21

Mojo Writing

Don't expect the Messiah.

There was an elaborate and meticulous prosecutor with the Special Prosecutors with an earthly humanity and well-balanced sense it felt like he will be right person for any job. People expected such persons like him could lead very successfully the Public Prosecution busy making a connection with politics power. But after the founding of Bahk Gunhey Administration, he moved out to one of a big law firms as an attorney.

He is still enthusiastic about his job with a high salary. We have to repine why those like him could not stay at the prosecution longer. Even at this moment the prosecution is towards escalating their investigation, it is sad to think that if the prosecution has armed themselves with a strict criteria, things would not ended up here.

practice	Do not expect the Messiah.
mojo	**Don't expect the Messiah.**
	[tip] 제목에서 마침표를 생략한다.
practice	There was ~~one~~ special prosecutor who is elaborate and meticulous.
	[Suggestion] one → a
mojo	**There was an elaborate and meticulous prosecutor with the Special.**
	[tip] **with the Special** 특수부 소속

text	구수한 인간미에 균형 감각도 갖춰 어떤 일을 맡아도 소임을 다할 것 같았다.
try	
	[word] 구수한 인간미 **nice humanity**　소임·임무 **one's duty**　다하다 **fulfill**

text	정치 권력에 줄대기가 잦은 검찰을 저런 이들이 이끌면 기대를 걸어도 되지 않을까 생각하곤 했다.
try	
	[word] 정치 권력 **political power**　줄대기 **connection with**　생각하다 **deem**

text	하지만 박근혜 정부 출범 이후 그는 대형 로펌의 변호사로 옮겼다.
try	
	[word] 정부 **admiration**　대형 로펌 **a big law firm**　변호사 **attorney** 옮기다 **move out**

practice

With his nice ~~humanity possessed~~ sense of balance, he would be looked like letting his duty to fulfill.

[Suggestion] **humanity possessed → humanity with possessed**

mojo

Prosecutors with an earthly humanity and well-balanced sense it felt like he will be right person for any job.

[tip] **Prosecutors** 특수부 **anearthly humanity** 세속적인 인간성 **well-balanced sense** 균형 감각을 갖춘 **right person** 맞는 사람

---

practice

~~It~~ would ~~be~~ deem~~ed~~ to expect let him to lead the prosecution in which frequently connecting with politic power.

[Suggestion] **it would be deemed → we would deem**

mojo

People expected such persons like him could lead verysuccessfully the Public Prosecution busy making a connection with politics power.

[tip] **the successful the Public Prosecution** 잘 나가는 검사

---

practice

But after starting Bahk Gunhey admiration, he moved out to one of big law firms as an attorney.

[Suggestion] **starting Bahk → starting of Bahk**

mojo

But after the founding of Bahk Gunhey Administration, he moved out to one of a big law firms as an attorney.

[tip] **after the founding of** 출범 이후 **as an attorney** 변호사로

text

여전히 작업에 열심이고 높은 연봉을 받지만 대한민국 검찰에 그와 같은
이들이 왜 남아 있을 수 없었는지 안타깝다.

try

[word] 여전히 열심이고 **still endeavor**

---

text

박대통령과 측근들에 대한 수사가 한창인 요즘, 검찰이 추상 같은 잣대로
무장했더라면 이 지경이 됐을까 싶어 아쉬움이 더 크다.

try

[word] 박대통령과 측근들 **President Bahk and her aids**
추상 같은 · 매우 엄격한 잣대로 **with strict measuring**

practice

He still endeavors his work and gets a lot of payment, yet we are sorry how ~~rarely~~ capable person stays in the Korean Prosecutor.

[Suggestion] how rarely → how few

mojo

He is still enthusiastic about his job with a high salary. We have to repine why those like him could not stay at the prosecution longer.

[tip] still enthusiastic 여전히 열정적이다 **with a high salary** 높은 연봉

repine 한탄하다 · 안타깝다

---

practice

~~Latest~~ amid the investigation in full against President Bahk and her aids, if prosecutor would arm with strict measuring, this situation wouldn't have come today.

[Suggestion] latest → recently

mojo

Even at this moment the prosecution is towards escalating their investigation, it is sad to think that if the prosecution has armed themselves with a strict criteria, things would not ended up here.

[tip] A strict criteria 추상 같은 잣대로 · 기준 · 평가

would not ended up here 이것으로 끝나지 않았을 것이다

✏️

아베의 트럼프 전략

아베 신조 일본 총리는 지난 9월 유엔 방문 때
뉴욕에서 힐러리 클린턴 민주당 대선 후보를 만났다.
힐러리가 아베의 숙소를 방문하는 형식이었다.
대선 격전지인 오하이오주에 일본계 기업이 많이 있는 점을 겨냥한
힐러리의 선거 전략이라는 얘기가 나왔다.
아베로서는 힐러리 당선에 대비하는 측면이 있었다.
당시는 힐러리가 도널드 트럼프 공화당 후보를 근소하게 앞서던 때였다.
아베는 동시에 트럼프 진영 거물급 인사도 비밀리에 만났다.
상무장관에 지명된 투자가 윌버 로스였다.
로스는 일본과 연이 깊은 지일파로 알려져 있다.
아베는 환태평양경제동반자협정(TPP)에 대한 이해를 구했다고 한다.
트럼프 당선 이후 공개된 사실이다.
로스는 원래 TPP 찬성파였지만
지금은 트럼프의 반대 입장에 보조를 맞추고 있다.
일본 외교의 치밀한 일면이 드러나는 대목이다.
아베의 TPP에 대한 집착은 대단하다.

text	아베의 트럼프 전략
try	

[word] 아베 **Abe**　전략 **strategiy**

22

Abe's Trump strategy

When Japanese Prime Minister Shinzo Abe visited U.N. in last September, he met Democrat candidate, Hillary Clinton in New York. Their meeting was arranged in the form of Hillary visiting Abe's accommodations. Hillary has brought up her campaign strategy targeting Ohio, the grand battle place,home to Japanese enterprises. Abe got some specific policy in mind for the possible election of Hillary Clinton. Hillary edged out her opposing candidate Trump by small margin then.

Abe also met some powerful figures around Trump Campaign camp in secrecy. It was investor Wilbur Ross, has been named as secretary of commerce in Trump administration. Ross is well known as a pro-Japanese with close tie to Japan. It is made public that Abe then asked him to examine carefully the interest in Trans-Pacific Partnership. This fact has been let out after Trump's election. Ross was the advocate of TPP, but he disapproves of the TPP at the same pace with Trump. The parts of the stories disclose that Japanese politics is a meticulous. Abe has a strong obsession forTPP.

practice	Abe's strategic plan counting Trump.
mojo	**Abe's Trump strategy**

<table>
<tr><td>text</td><td>아베 신조 일본 총리는 지난 9월 유엔 방문 때 뉴욕에서 힐러리 클린턴 민주당 대선 후보를 만났다.</td></tr>
<tr><td>try</td><td></td></tr>
</table>

[word] 일본 총리 **Japanese Prime Minister** 힐러리 클린턴 **Hillary Clinton**
민주당 대선 후보 **Democratic presidential nominee**

<table>
<tr><td>text</td><td>힐러리가 아베의 숙소를 방문하는 형식이었다.</td></tr>
<tr><td>try</td><td></td></tr>
</table>

[word] 숙소 **accommodation**

<table>
<tr><td>text</td><td>대선 격전지인 오하이오주에 일본계 기업이 많이 있는 점을 겨냥한 힐러리의 선거 전략이라는 얘기가 나왔다.</td></tr>
<tr><td>try</td><td></td></tr>
</table>

[word] 대선 격전지 **battle ground of presidential election** 일본계 기업
Japanese enterprises 선거 전략 **campaign strategy**

practice

Japanese Prime Minister Shinzo Abe met the Democratic presidential nominee Hillary Clinton ~~at~~ New York, visiting U.N. last September.

[Suggestion] at New York → in New York Clinton visiting U.N. last September in New York

mojo

When Japanese Prime Minister Shinzo Abe visited U.N. in last September, he met Democrat candidate, Hillary Clinton in New York.

[tip] when Shinzo Abe visited U.N. 아베가 유엔 방문 때

he met Democrat candidate 그는 민주당 대선 후보를 만났다

---

practice

It was ~~done~~ that Hillary visited Abe's place.

[Suggestion] it was arranged in the way that

mojo

Their meeting was arranged in the form of Hillary visiting Abe's accommodations.

[tip] Their meeting was arranged 미팅이 마련되었다

in the form of visiting 방문하는 형식으로

---

practice

It was aimed including a strategic campaign of Hillary that the state of Ohio, ~~where has~~ many Japanese companies, a fierce battle ground, medias said.

[Suggestion] where has → which there are

mojo

Hillary has brought up her campaign strategy targeting Ohio, the grand battle place, home to Japanese enterprises.

[tip] the grand battle place, (which is) home to Japanese enterprises

일본계 기업이 많은 대선 격전지

text	아베로서는 힐러리 당선에 대비하는 측면이 있었다. 당시는 힐러리가 도널드 트럼프 공화당 후보를 근소하게 앞서던 때였다.
try	

[word] 대비하는 · 염두에 두다 · 고려하다 · 마음에 두다 **in mind**

공화당 후보 **Republican candidate** 근소하게 **a little**

---

text	아베는 동시에 트럼프 진영 거물급 인사도 비밀리에 만났다. 상무장관에 지명된 투자가 윌버 로스였다. 로스는 일본과 연이 깊은 지일파로 알려져 있다.
try	

[word] 동시에 **simultaneously** 트럼프 진영 **Trump campaign camp**

거물급 인사 **tycoon** 상무장관 **secretary of commerce**

---

text	아베는 환태평양경제동반자협정(TPP)에 대한 이해를 구했다고 한다. 트럼프 당선 이후 공개된 사실이다.
try	

[word] 환태평양경제동반자협정 **TPP · Trans-Pacific partnership**

practice For Abe, it ~~was posed in part to elect of Hillary Clinton~~ when she was leading a little on the Republican candidate Donald Trump.

[Suggestion] **it posed for Hillary Clinton to be elected as president**

mojo Abe got some specific policy in mind for the possible election of Hillary Clinton. Hillary edged out her opposing candidate Trump by small margin then.

[tip] **Some specific policy in mind** 대비하는 측면

Hillary edged out 힐러리가 근소하게 앞서다

---

practice Simultaneously, Abe met even a few tycoons of Trump camp secretly. It was Wilbur Ross, ~~who appointed~~ investor as a Trump's secretary of commerce and is known ~~for~~ pro-Japan with tight ties.

[Suggestion] **Who appointed → who was appointed for pro-Japan with tight ties → pro-Japan with tight ties**

mojo Abe also met some powerful figures around Trump campaign camp in secrecy.It was investor Wilbur Ross, who has been named as secretary of commerce in Trump administration.Ross is well known as a pro-Japanese with close tie to Japan.

[tip] **named as secretary of commerce in Trump administration** 트럼프 행정부에서 상무장관으로 임명된

---

practice Abe ~~then asked to understand his idea on~~ Trans-Pacific partnership, it was revealed true after Trump winning.

[tip] **then asked to understand his idea on → then him asked to understand his interest in TPP**

mojo It is made public that Abe then asked him to examine carefully the interest in Trans-Pacific Partnership.not ended up here.

[tip] **be well known** 잘 알려지다 **close tie to** 밀접한 유대

interest in 관심을 가지다

로스는 원래 TPP 찬성파였지만 지금은 트럼프의 반대 입장에 보조를 맞추고 있다.

[word] 찬성 **support·approval** 반대 **oppose·against**

일본 외교의 치밀한 일면이 드러나는 대목이다. 아베의 TPP에 대한 집착은 대단하다.

[word] 집착 **stick for**

practice	Ross had assented to TPP originally, and then he is opposing to it in line with Trump's stance. **[Suggestion] in line with Trump's stance**
mojo	Ross was the advocate of TPP, but he disapproves of the TPP at the same pace with Trump. This fact has been let out after Trump's election. **[tip] the advocate of TPP TPP 옹호 at the same pace with Trump 트럼프와 같은 보조에서 the fact has been let out 공개된 사실**
practice	It is found partly for Japan to endeavor in their diplomacy. Abe has significantly stuck for TPP.
mojo	The parts of the stories disclose that Japanese politics is a meticulous. Abe has a strong obsession for TPP. **[tip] obsession for 집념**

가스요금까지 5.6% 뛰어 생활물가 2년 만에 최고

생활물가가 2년 4개월 만에 가장 큰 폭으로 올랐다.
배추나 무, 파 같은 신선식품 값이 급등했고
도시가스 요금도 올랐다.
1일 통계청이 낸 '11월 소비자물가 동향'에 따르면
지난달 생활물가 상승률은 전년 동월 대비 1.1%를 기록했다.
2014년 7월 1.4% 이후 가장 높은 수치다.
통계청은 소비자가 자주 구입하는 142개 품목을 추려 생활물가지수를 낸다.
이 지수가 2년여 만에 최고치로 올라갔다는 것은
소비자가 체감하는 물가 사정이 그만큼 나빠졌다는 의미다.

text	가스요금까지 5.6% 뛰어 생활물가 2년 만에 최고
try	
	[word] 가스요금 **gas rate** 생활물가 **living price**

text	생활물가가 2년 4개월 만에 가장 큰 폭으로 올랐다.
try	
	[word] 2년 4개월 만에 **over two years and four months** 오르다 **rise**

Mojo Writing

Since gas rate also has jumped up 5.6%, living price topped in two years.

Even gas rate has gone up 5.6% and living price hit the highest in two years. The prices have gone up over two years and four months by the widest margin. The fresh food prices such as cabbage, radish and welsh onion have surged and so did city gas rate. According to consumer price index of last November released by National Statistic Office on the first day, the ratio of living prices rising over the last month was recorded 1.1% compared with that of last year. It is the highest figures since 1.4% recorded in the July of 2014. The Statistic Office surveys 142 items of consumer favorites and sorts the price index. The index hitting a new high means that the prices consumers feel have gone from bad to worse.

practice	Since gas rate also has jumped up 5.6%, living price topped in two years. **[Suggestion] has jumped up (by) 5.8%**
mojo	Even gas rate has gone up 5.6% and living price hit the highest in two years. **[tip] hit the highest 최고 높이에 달하다**
practice	The price rose up the biggest size in 4 months and 2 years. **[Suggestion] in 4 months and 2 years → in 2 years and 4 months**
mojo	The prices have gone up over two years and four months by the widest margin. **[tip] by the widest margin 가장 큰 폭으로**

text	배추나 무, 파 같은 신선식품 값이 급등했고 도시가스 요금도 올랐다
try	
	[word] 배추 **cabbage** 무 **radish** 파 **leek · welsh onion** 신선식품 **fresh food**

text	1일 통계청이 낸 '11월 소비자물가 동향'에 따르면 지난달 생활물가 상승률은 전년 동월 대비 1.1%를 기록했다.
try	
	[word] 통계청 **National Statistic Office** 소비자물가 동향 **the consumer price index** 기록하다 **record**

text	2014년 7월 1.4% 이후 가장 높은 수치다.
try	
	[word] 2014년 7월 **July of 2014**

text	통계청은 소비자가 자주 구입하는 142 개 품목을 추려 생활물가지수를 낸다.
try	
	[word] 소비자 **consumer** 자주 **often · frequently** 추려내다 **sort out**

| **practice** | The fresh food's price such as cabbage, radish and, surged, and so did city gas. |
| **mojo** | The fresh food prices such as cabbage, radish and leek have surged and so did city gas rate. |

[tip] have surged 올랐다 **so did city gas rate** 도시가스 요금도 그렇다

---

practice On the first day, according to 'the consumer price index of National Statistic Office,' last month's living price rising rate recorded 1.1% compare ~~to~~ same month of last year.

[Suggestion] compare to → compare with

mojo According to the consumer price indexof last November released by National Statistic Office on the first day, the ratio of living prices rising over the last month was recorded 1.1% compared with that of last year.

[tip] over the last month 지난달 전반 **the ratio of living prices rising** 생활물가 상승률

---

practice It is the highest figures, after 1.4% ~~on July 2014~~.

[Suggestion] on July 2014 → in the July of 2014

mojo It is the highest figures since 1.4% recorded in the July of 2014.

[tip] since 1.4% recorded 1.4% 기록 이후

---

practice The statistic office surveyed 142 items of consuming frequently and computed ~~to~~ the index.

[Suggestion] computedto the index → computed the index

mojo The Statistic Office surveys 142 items of consumer favorites and sorts the price index.

[tip] consumer favorites 소비자 선호 · 자주 구입하는

text

이 지수가 2년여 만에 최고치로 올라갔다는 것은 소비자가 체감하는 물가 사정이 그만큼 나빠졌다는 의미다.

try

[word] 체감하는 물가 **the price which is consumers feel**

<table>
<tr><td>practice</td><td>When it surged at the highest in 2 years, it shows the price <s>of consumer's sensibility</s> worse.

[Suggestion] **The price of consumer's sensibility** 소비자 감성가격이 →

the prices (which are) consumers feel 소비자가 느끼는 물가가격</td></tr>
<tr><td>mojo</td><td>The index hitting a new high means that the prices consumers feel have gone from bad to worse.

[tip] **have gone from bad to worse** 나빠졌다</td></tr>
</table>

✎

"갑자기 시력 잃은 국가대표 사연 라디오서 듣고 시나리오 만들었죠"

"잘 나가던 국가대표가 시력을 잃는다면 그 마음은 어떤 것일까.
'형'의 시나리오는 그렇게 시작됐죠."
23일 서울의 한 극장.
강단에 선 유영아(42) 작가의 말에
온 청중의 시선이 쏠렸다.
그가 각본을 쓴 영화 '형'(권수경 감독)의 개봉을 맞아,
한국콘텐츠진흥원 창의인재동반사업의 일환으로 진행된
특강 자리였다.
창작 지망생들을 지원하는 이 사업의 멘토로 활동 중인 그는
'7번 방의 선물'로 천만 작가의 반열에 올랐다.

text	"갑자기 시력 잃은 국가대표 사연 라디오서 듣고 시나리오 만들었죠"
try	[word] 갑자기 **all of sudden**　시력 잃은 국가대표 **a national athlete (who is) lost his eyesight**　시나리오 **scenario**
text	"잘나가던 국가대표가 시력을 잃는다면 그 마음은 어떤 것일까. '형'의 시나리오는 그렇게 시작됐죠."
try	[word] 잘나가던 국가대표 **a successful nationalathlete** 그 마음은 어떤 것일까 **how might he feel it?**

Mojo Writing

I have simply put some tweaks on the above writing.

"Right after I heard over the radio that a national athlete lost his eyesight, I wrote the scenario."
"If a successful national athlete lost his eyesight, how might he feel it? The scenario about you has started to go that way."
In the one of theater on November 23rd in Seoul, most of the audience turned their eyes upon the remark of writer Yu Youngah standing on the platform. Greeting a release of the movie "Brother" directed by Kwom Sookyung, her speech was specially designed for as a part of Talent Program for Korea Creative Contents Development. Acting as mentor for the business supporting the literary aspirants, she took her place among 10 millions of authors with her work, 'gifts of 7th Room.'

practice	"The scenario was started to write since I heard a story of a national athlete lost his sight all of sudden ~~through~~ radio." **[Suggestion] through radio → on radio**
mojo	"Right after I heard over the radio that a national athlete lost his eyesight, I wrote the scenario." **[tip] hit the highest** 최고 높이에 달하다
practice	"What is a mind when an athlete ~~being made name~~ lost his sight. The scenario of "The Brother" was begun from that.". **[Suggestion] being made name → with good name**
mojo	"If a successful national athlete lost his eyesight, how might he feel it? The scenario of "The Brother"has started to go that way." **[tip] has started to go that way** 그렇게 시작됐다

text	23일 서울의 한 극장. 강단에 선 유영아(42) 작가의 말에 온 청중의 시선이 쏠렸다.
try	
[word]	극장 **theater**　강단 **platform**　작가 **author · writer**　청중 **audience** 시선 **eyes**
text	그가 각본을 쓴 영화 '형'(권수경 감독)의 개봉을 맞아, 한국콘텐츠진흥원 창의인재동반사업의 일환으로 진행된 특강 자리였다.
try	
[word]	각본 · 원고 **scenario**　감독 **move director**　개봉 **opening**　한국콘텐츠진흥원 **Korea Creative Content Agency**　특강 **special speech**
text	창작 지망생들을 지원하는 이 사업의 멘토로 활동중인 그는 '7번방의 선물'로 천만 작가의 반열에 올랐다.
try	
[word]	창작 지망생 **literary aspirant**　멘토 · 조언자 **mentor**　반열 **rank**

practice	On 23 of November in one theater of Seoul, many audience's eyes focused on Yu Youngah, 42 author, standing on stage. [Suggestion] 42 author, standing on stage → 42 author standing on stage
mojo	In the one of theater on November 23rd in Seoul, most of the audience turned their eyes upon the remark of writer Yu Youngah standing on the platform. [tip] most of the audience turned their eyes upon 대부분의 청중의 시선이 쏠렸다

practice	Greeting for disclosing movie of THE BROTHER ~~that she wrote the scenario~~ and Guwon SooKyong directed it, a special speech staged by one of parts of Creative companied talent Business from Korea Creative Content Agency. [Suggestion] that she wrote the scenario → that the scenario she wrote
mojo	Greeting a release of the movie "The Brother" directed by Kwom Sookyung, her speech was specially designed for as a part of Talent Program for Korea Creative Contents Development. [tip] was specially designed for 진행된 · 마련된

practice	Acting as a mentor ~~of~~ this business supporting literary aspirants, she ranked in order of the ten million authors with "The gift of 7TH Room". [Suggestion] as a mentor this business
mojo	Acting as mentor for the business supporting the literary aspirants, she took her place among 10 millions of authors with her work, "The Gifts of 7th Room." [tip] took her place 그녀의 입지를 취한 · 반열에 오른 · 위치를 차지하다

지상작전사령부 2018년 창설,
전작권 환수 속도 높인다

육군 1·3군 통합, 국방개혁 본격화
유사시 한 · 미연합군 지상작전 지휘
연합사 미군, 단계적으로 지작사 이동
내년 완전한 합동근무 체제 구축

국방부가 전시작전통제권 전환과
국방개혁의 핵심인
지상작전사령부 (지작사)를 2018년 8~11월 창설키로 하고
본격적인 준비작업에 들어갔다.
28일 군 관계자에 따르면 국방부는
경기도 용인에 위치한 제3야전군 사령부 내에
지작사 관련 시설을 지난달 완공했다.
이달 들어서는 '임시 지작사' 구성에 들어갔다.
지작사는 육군 1·3군 사령부를 통합한 사령부로
유사시에는 한반도 지상작전을 지휘하는
연합지상구성군사령부(GCC: Ground Component Command) 기능을
수행한다.
국방부는 2014년 '국방개혁 2014~2030'을 발표하면서
상세한 지작사 창설 계획은 공개하지 않았다.

Ground operational headquarters will be founded in 2018. The transfer of war time operational control from the U.S. will gain in speed.

The army 1·3 corps are consolidated into one.
The national defense reform will be regularized.
In time of emergency, the Korea-U.S. combined Forces will take command of the ground operation.
The U.S. forces of the combined headquarters will be moving the operational headquarters by stages, and coming to overhaul the system into a complete joint service structure.

The national defense has begun planning to set up a headquarters for the transfer of wartime operational control and the ground operation command to the point of national defense reform between August and November 2018, and started working to get them prepared.
According to Korean army concerned, the national defense has completed installationsrelated to the ground operation within the headquarters of Korean 3rd field army last month.
This month they turned their effort into setting up a provisional headquarters of ground operation.
As a command headquarters with consolidation of Korean Army 1·3 corps, the ground operation headquarters will carry out its duty as Ground Component Command, which will control a ground operation on Korean peninsula in an emergency.
In the 2014 national defense reform '2014~2030,' the department of national defense did not open a detailed schedule for the founding of the ground operation command to the public.

text	지상작전사령부 2018년 창설, 전작권 환수 속도 높인다
try	[word] 지상작전사령부 **Ground operational headquarters** 창설 **found** 전작권 · 전시작전통제권 **Wartime Operational Control** 환수 **transfer**
text	육군 1·3군 통합, 국방개혁 본격화
try	[word] 육군 1·3군 **the army 1·3 corps** 국방개혁 **the national defense reform**
text	유사시 한 · 미연합군 지상작전 지휘
try	[word] 유사시 **in emergency** 한 · 미연합군 **the Korea-U.S. combined Forces** 지상작전 **the ground operation**

practice ~~It will be founded an headquarters of ground operation~~ in 2018, raising speed of the Transition of Wartime Operational Control clawing back this country.

[Suggestion] an headquarters of ground operation will be founded

mojo Ground operational headquarters will be founded in 2018. The transfer of war time operational control from the U.S. will gain in speed.

[tip] will gain in speed 속도를 높인다

---

practice Unifying of military 1·3 forces, ~~it~~ is full-fledged for reforming of national defense.

[Suggestion] for reforming of national defense is full-fledged

mojo The army 1·3 corps are consolidated into one. The national defense reform will be regularized.

[tip] corps 군단 **be consolidated into one · join or combine together into one thing** 통합되다 **regularize** 본격화하다 · 규칙적으로 하다

---

practice In national emergency, the ROK-U.S. Combined Forces ~~direct~~ ground operation.

[Suggestion] Combined Forces direct ground operation

→ Combined Forces ground operation

mojo In time of emergency, the Korea-U.S. combined Forces will take command of the ground operation.

[tip] In time of emergency 유사시에 **take command** 지휘하다

text

연합사 미군, 단계적으로 지작사 이동
내년 완전한 합동근무 체제 구축

try

[word] 이동 move

text

국방부가 전시작전통제권 전환과 국방개혁의 핵심인 지상작전사령부 (지작사)
를 2018년 8~11월 창설키로 하고 본격적인 준비작업에 들어갔다.

try

[word] 개혁 reform 핵심 key · point 창설 found · create
준비작업 preliminary work

practice

The part of U.S. of the Combined Forces ~~will gradually~~ to the Headquarters. Until next year the system of entire join operation will be completed.

[Suggestion] will gradually → will move gradually

move out → move in 이사 들어가다

mojo

The U.S. forces of the combined headquarters will be moving the operational headquarters by stages, and coming to overhaul the system into a complete joint service structure.

[tip] will be moving 이동될 것이다   **by stages** 단계적으로

---

practice

With being founded Ground Operational ~~Headquarters~~, which is transferring of war time operational control and a key of the national defense reform, ~~between August and November in 2018~~, Defense Ministry has begun to enter preliminary work.

[Suggestion] headquarters between August and November in 2018, which

mojo

The national defense has begun planning to set up a headquarters for the transfer of wartime operational control and the ground operation command to the point of national defense reform between August and November 2018, and started working to get them prepared.

[tip] set up a headquarters 사령부를 창설하다   **the point of national defense reform** 국방개혁의 핵심   **working to get them prepared** 본격적인 준비작업

text

28일 군 관계자에 따르면 국방부는 경기도 용인에 위치한 제3야전군 사령부 내에 지작사 관련 시설을 지난달 완공했다. 이달 들어서는 '임시 지작사' 구성에 들어갔다.

try

[word] 군관계자 **military official** 제3야전군 사령부 **the headquarters of Korean 3rd field army** 임시 지작사 **preliminary GCC**

text

지작사는 육군 1·3군 사령부를 통합한 사령부로 유사시에는 한반도 지상작전을 지휘하는 연합지상구성군사령부 기능을 수행한다.

try

[word] 연합지상구성군사령부 **GCC · Ground Component Command** 수행한다 **perform**

practice

According to a military official on November 28, the ministry constructed some facilities relating with the ground operational headquarters in the third field army placed in Yongin, Kyonggi province. In the month, ~~they already~~ entered to consist of 'preliminary headquarters of ground operation.'

[Suggestion] they already → they have already

mojo

According to Korean army concerned, the national defense has completed installations related to the ground operation within the headquarters of Korean 3rd field army last month. This month they turned their effort into setting up a provisional headquarters of ground operation.

[tip] **Korean army concerned** 군관계자 **installation related to the ground operation** 지작사 관련 시설 **a provisional headquarters of ground operation** 임시 지상작전사령부

---

practice

The headquarters of ground operation ~~is~~ performedas a combined command headquarters with Korean Army 1·3 corps, if Korean peninsula happens something in risk, then it will conduct a command.

[Suggestion] is performed as → has been performed

mojo

As a command headquarters with consolidation of Korean Army 1·3 corps, the ground operation headquarters will carry out its duty as Ground Component Command, which will control a ground operation on Korean peninsula in an emergency.

[tip] **As a command headquarters with consolidation** 통한된 사령부로서 **carry out its duty** 임무를 수행하다

국방부는 2014년 '국방개혁 2014~2030'을 발표하면서 상세한 지작사 창설 계획은 공개하지 않았다.

[word] 국방부 the department of national defense

practice

~~Even~~ if Defense ministry reported 'Reform of defense 2014~2030', they kept covered the plan of GCC.

[Suggestion] even → while · when

mojo

In the 2014 national defense reform '2014-2030,' the department of national defense did not open a detailed schedule for the founding of the ground operation command to the public.

[tip] **did not open a detailed schedule** 상세한 계획은 공개하지 않았다

✏️

당신의 바닥은 누군가의 하늘?

쓰레기통 앞에 한 소녀가 추위에 떨고 있다.

작고 여리지만, 당차고 의욕적이다.

작은 공간을 헤집으며 살기 위해 발버둥치고 있는 소녀 앞에 나타난 속칭 된장녀.

선베드(sunbed)에 몸을 싣고 한 것 여유를 부린다.

그의 세상에는 고급 잔디 융단이 깔려 있다.

쓰레기통과 선베드, 소녀와 된장녀.

'있는 자와 없는 자'로 이분된 사회의 한 단면이다.

여기에 일용직 근로자와 목욕가운 차림의 남자가 등장하면서

인간 계층은 더욱 복잡하게 얽히기 시작한다.

그들은 더 높은 곳을 차지하려고 서로를 짓밟고 무너뜨리기를 반복한다.

머리싸움과 몸싸움이 무서우리만큼 치열하다.

text	당신의 바닥은 누군가의 하늘?
try	[word] 바닥 **bottom**
text	쓰레기통 앞에 한 소녀가 추위에 떨고 있다.
try	[word] 쓰레기통 **trash can**
text	작고 여리지만, 당차고 의욕적이다.
try	[word] 작고 여리다 **little and young**

26

Mojo Writing

Your bottom is the heaven for someone else?

In front of trash bin, a girl is shivering in the cold. She is little, but sturdy and motivated. A Toenjang-Nyo, 'soybean-paste girl' in Korean, showed up in front of the girl, struggling to live through a little space. Placing her body on the sunbed, she is full calm and at ease. Her world is covered with a classy lawn carpet.
The trash bin and sunbed, Toenjang-Nyo and a girl are a phase of our society that is bisected into the have and have-not.
A daily worker and a man in bathing gown showing up here, the human stratum begins to get complicated. They struggle to grab higher place, trying to tremble and override each other. The brain and body war will get on moving hard.

practice	Is it a heaven for someone, where's a floor for you?
mojo	**Your bottom is the heaven for someone else?**
	[tip] **Your bottom someone else** 당신이 아닌 타인
practice	In front of trashcan, there is a girl ~~trembling~~ on cold.
	[Suggestion] **trembling** 두려움에떨다 → **shivering** 추위에 떨다
mojo	**In front of trash bin, a girl is shivering in the cold.**
	[tip] **shivering in the cold**
practice	Even now she is little and young, but bold and motivated..
mojo	**She is little, but sturdy and motivated.**
	[tip] **sturdy and motivated** 당차고 의욕적

<table>
<tr><td>text</td><td>작은 공간을 헤집으며 살기 위해 발버둥치고 있는 소녀 앞에 나타난 속칭 된장녀. 선베드(sunbed)에 몸을 싣고 한 것 여유를 부린다.</td></tr>
<tr><td>try</td><td></td></tr>
<tr><td></td><td>[word] 선베드 sunbed</td></tr>
</table>

<table>
<tr><td>text</td><td>그의 세상에는 고급 잔디 융단이 깔려 있다.</td></tr>
<tr><td>try</td><td></td></tr>
<tr><td></td><td>[word] 고급 high quality　융단 carpet</td></tr>
</table>

<table>
<tr><td>text</td><td>쓰레기통과 선베드, 소녀와 된장녀. '있는 자와 없는 자'로 이분된 사회의 한 단면이다.</td></tr>
<tr><td>try</td><td></td></tr>
<tr><td></td><td>[word]선베드 sunbed　된장녀 Toenjang-Nyo　이분된다 divided</td></tr>
</table>

<table>
<tr><td>text</td><td>여기에 일용직 근로자와 목욕가운 차림의 남자가 등장하면서 인간 계층은 더욱 복잡하게 얽히기 시작한다.</td></tr>
<tr><td>try</td><td></td></tr>
<tr><td></td><td>[word] 일용직 근로자 day job · temporary job · pay labor</td></tr>
</table>

practice	~~So called~~ "a pasted soybean girl" is appeared before her struggling to live digging up in small space. The soybean girl is gesturing full of her arrogance putting her body on sunbed. **[Suggestion] so called → so-called**
mojo	A Toenjang-Nyo, 'soybean-paste girl' in Korean, showed up in front of the girl, struggling to live through a little space. Placing her body on the sunbed, she is full calm and at ease. **[tip] soybean-paste girl'inKorean through a little spaceis full calm and at ease** 한껏
practice	There is spread luxury sod like carpet ~~in~~ everywhere her field. **[Suggestion] like carpet in everywhere → like carpet everywhere**
mojo	Her world is covered with a classy lawn carpet. **[tip] a classy lawn carpet**
practice	Such as a Trashcan and a sunbed, a girl and a soybean girl, as well as the have and have not, all of those are a profile of our dichotomized society.
mojo	The trash bin and sunbed, Toenjang-Nyo and a girl are a phase of our society that is bisected into the have and have-not. **[tip] the have and have-not bisected** 갈라진 · 양분된
practice	Here, with staging up both a daily worker and a man ~~dressed~~ in bathrobe, the community of human being begins to tangle further intricately. **[Suggestion] a man dressed in bathrobe → a man in bathrobe**
mojo	A daily worker and a man in bathing gown showing up here, the human stratum beginsto get complicated. **[tip] the human stratum to get complicated**

그들은 더 높은 곳을 차지하려고 서로를 짓밟고 무너뜨리기를 반복한다.
머리싸움과 몸싸움이 무서우리만큼 치열하다.

[word] 차지하다 occupy · hold

그들은 더 높은 곳을 차지하려고 서로를 짓밟고 무너뜨리기를 반복한다.
머리싸움과 몸싸움이 무서우리만큼 치열하다.

They are going on trampling and overriding of each other trying to grab higher than the other part. Their battle of brain and body makes horror as much as a move tooth and nail.

They struggle to grab higher place, trying to tremble and override each other. The brain and body war will get on moving hard.

[tip] get on moving hard

최고에게만 허락된 자리

누구나 최고를 꿈꿀 수 있지만
아무나 오를 수 없는 자리가 있습니다.
"올곧은 경영철학과 앞서 가는 리더십으로
빠른 성과보다는 바른 경영을 실천하는 사람.
정상의 자리에서도 도전을 멈추지 않고
혁신과 열정의 초심을 지금까지 이어가는 사람.
대한민국 경영의 가장 영광스러운 자리에 오른
2016 한국의 경영대상 기업들입니다."
오랜 시간 우리 경제의 든든한 힘이 되어 준 당신은
대한민국의 자랑스러운 경영 경쟁력입니다.

text	최고에게만 허락된 자리
try	
	[word] 자리 **place** 허락되다 **be allowed**

text	누구나 최고를 꿈꿀 수 있지만 아무나 오를 수 없는 자리가 있습니다.
try	
	[word] 누구나 **everybody** 꿈꾸다 **have dream**

27

Mojo Writing

The place where is allowed only to top

Everyone can dream the best, yet there is a position which anyone can't raise.

The man who prefers putting a right management into a practice to a fast performance, with a righteous management philosophy and advanced leadership, the man who can never stop his challenge even when he is on top position, bringing about an innovation and remembering the ardor, with which he felt who he first began, It is Korean companies who have been awarded business management grand prizes, coming up on these places of the honor in the year of 2016.

You have been a sturdy energy for our economy and a proudly competitiveness in Korean businesses.

practice	The post what is allowed to a top
mojo	The place where is allowed only to top [tip] **only to top** 최고에게만

practice	Everybody could ~~have~~ dream to be a top, but there is a seat nobody raised up easily. [Suggestion] **could have dream → could dream**
mojo	Everyone can dream the best, yet there is a position which anyone can't rise. [tip] **can dream the best, yet** 최고를 꿈꿀 수 있지만 **which anyone can't rise** 쉽게 오르지 못하는

text

"올곧은 경영철학과 앞서 가는 리더십으로
빠른 성과보다는 바른 경영을 실천하는 사람.
정상의 자리에서도 도전을 멈추지 않고
혁신과 열정의 초심을 지금까지 이어가는 사람.

try

[word] 올곧은 경영철학 **right management** 리더십 **leadership**
빠른 성과 **speedy outcome** 실천하다 **practice** 정상의 자리 **the place of top**
도전 **challenge** 혁신 **innovation** 열정 **passion** 초심 **one's original intention**

text

대한민국 경영의 가장 영광스러운 자리에 오른
2016 한국의 경영대상 기업들입니다."

try

[word] 영광스러운 자리 **these places of the honor**
경영대상 **management prize**

<table>
<tr><td>practice</td><td>

As the right managing philosophy and advancing leadership, a man prefers putting in practice right management to speedy outcome.

~~With unstoppable~~ challenging even at the top post, a man has led original intention by reform and passion so far.

[Suggestion] with unstoppable → without stopping challenging

</td></tr>
<tr><td>mojo</td><td>

The man who prefers putting a right management into a practice to a fast performance, with a righteous management philosophy and advanced leadership, the man who can never stop his challenge even when he is on top position, bringing about an innovation and remembering the ardor, with which he felt who he first began.

[tip] prefer A to B A를 더 선호하다 **advanced leadership** 앞서가는 리더십 **can never stop** 결코 멈추지 않는 **when he is on top position** 정상의 자리에서도 **bring about** 가져오다 · 이어가다

</td></tr>
</table>

<table>
<tr><td>practice</td><td>

Those are Korean companies awarded management prizes in 2016, rising up on the most honorable posts among Korean management businesses.

</td></tr>
<tr><td>mojo</td><td>

It is Korean companies who have been awarded business management grand prizes, coming up on these places of the honor in the year of 2016.

[tip] Business management Grand prizes 경영대상 **in the year of 2016** 2016년에

</td></tr>
</table>

text	오랜 시간 우리 경제의 든든한 힘이 되어 준 당신은 대한민국의 자랑스러운 경영 경쟁력입니다.
try	

[word] 든든한 힘 **strong power** 자랑스러운 경영 경쟁력 **proudly competitiveness**

practice   Have made strong power for our economy for a long time, you are competitive ~~power itself of getting pride~~ of Korea.

[Suggestion] **power itself of getting pride → power itself, pride**

mojo   You have been a sturdy energy for our economy and a proudly competitiveness in Korean businesses.

[tip] **have been a sturdy energy** 든든한 힘이 되다

에너지를 다시 생각합니다.

에너지를 만들고, 에너지를 저장하고,
에너지를 쓰는 방법을 다시 생각합니다.
인간과 인간, 인간과 자연이 함께 행복한 에너지를 위해–
그것은 이제 결코 먼 미래의 이야기가 아니라
오늘 이 시간, 우리 모두의 삶에 관한 문제이며
인류가 꼭 풀어야 할 과제이기 때문입니다.
우리의 더 나은 삶을 위해 LG의 에너지솔루션이 함께합니다.

text	에너지를 다시 생각합니다.
try	[word] 다시 생각합니다 **rethink**
text	에너지를 만들고, 에너지를 저장하고, 에너지를 쓰는 방법을 다시 생각합니다.
try	[word] 만들고 **make**　저장하고 **restore**　쓰는 방법 **way to use**

28

Mojo Writing

Rethink about the issues of energy.

All we ever think is how to make energy,
store it and make best of it.
For human and human, and human and nature to have the use of a
happy energy, it is not far away from, but it is about a matter of our
lives this time, and it requires our human being to solve.
For better our living, LG energy solution is going together.

practice	Rethink energy
mojo	**Rethink about the issues of energy.** [tip] **about the issues** 현안에 관해서
practice	We ~~need~~ think again to making energy, restoring it and using way of it. [Suggestion] **we need think → we think**
mojo	**All we ever think is how to make energy, store it and make best of it.** [tip] **make best** 잘 활용하다 · 쓰다

인간과 인간, 인간과 자연이 함께 행복한 에너지를 위해–
그것은 이제 결코 먼 미래의 이야기가 아니라
오늘 이 시간, 우리 모두의 삶에 관한 문제이며
인류가 꼭 풀어야 할 과제이기 때문입니다.

[word] 인간 **human being** 자연 **nature** 미래 **future** 삶 **life**
풀어야 할 과제 **problem to be solved**

우리의 더 나은 삶을 위해 LG의 에너지솔루션이 함께합니다.

[word] 더 나은 삶 **the better life** 에너지솔루션 **Energy Solution**

practice Human and human, and human being and nature all together, for happy using of energy, it is not only problems for future, but this time today our life problems ~~and a project to be solved problem~~ by human being.

[Suggestion] our life problems by human being

mojo For human and human, and human and nature to have the use of a happy energy, it is not far away from, but it is about a matter of our lives this time, and it requires our human being to solve.

[tip] for human ~ to have 인간과 인간, 인간과 자연이 행복한 에너지를 사용하기 위해 **not far away from** 먼 미래가 아니라 **requires human being to solve** 인류가 풀어야 할

---

practice For the further better our life, LG Energy Solution will be by your side together.

mojo For better our living, LG energy solution is going together.

[tip] is going together 함께가다

점원도 계산대도 없어… 아마존, AI편의점 첫선

시애틀서 '아마존 고' 시범 운영

스마트폰으로 계정 만들고 쇼핑

사고 싶은 물건 들고나가면 끝

업계선 쇼핑 혁명 신호탄 평가

쇼핑은 즐겁지만 계산대 앞에 줄을 선 뒤 일일이 물건을 꺼내

계산을 하는 과정은 지루하기 짝이 없다.

세계 최대 전자상거래 업체인 아마존이 사람은 없고

물건만 있는 '인공지능(AI) 편의점'을 선보인다.

오프라인 서점인 '아마존 서점'을 개설한 데 이어

소매점 시장으로 오프라인 영역을 확장시키려는 움직임이다.

아마존은 5일(현지시간) 미국 시애틀에 $167m^2$(약 50.5평) 규모의

상점 '아마존 고(Amazon Go)'를 오픈했다고 밝혔다.

아마존 고는 주로 식료품을 판매하는 편의점으로

우선 아마존 직원을 대상으로 시범 운영 한 뒤

내년 초 일반에 공개할 예정이다.

text	점원도 계산대도 없어… 아마존, AI편의점 첫선
try	

[word] 점원 **cashier** 계산대 **counter** AI 편의점 **Artificial Intelligent store**

29

Mojo Writing

Amazon first artificial intelligent store has neither cashier nor counter.

In Seattle 'Amazon go' is currently piloting the new store.
Making smartphone account, shopping what you want to buy, and then carrying, it simply ends up your shopping.
Business circles say it is a signal of shopping revolution.
Shopping is joyful, yet waiting in a long line in front of counter to compute all the prices is a quite boring process. The world biggest e-commerce, Amazon, is demonstrating AI convenient store to sell goods without any cashier.
It is moving to expand their on-line boundary into retail market.
Amazon, on local time this month 5th, announced that it opened 'Amazon Go' (167m square) in Chicago, according to Amazon.
Amazon Go is convenient store mainly selling foodstuffs. It first intends for its employees, and then will be open for the public early next year.

practice	There is no cashier and no counter that is shown first Artificial Intelligent store by Amazon.The world biggest on-line commerce, Amazon, ~~is shown~~ an AI Store that is stocked products without cashier. **[Suggestion] is shown → showing**
mojo	Amazon first artificial intelligent store has neither cashier nor counter. **[tip] has neither cashier nor counter** 점원도 계산대도 없다

text	시애틀서 '아마존 고' 시범 운영
try	[word] 시애틀 **Seattle** 아마존 고 **Amazon Go** 시범 운영 **run in pilot**
text	스마트폰으로 계정 만들고 쇼핑 사고 싶은 물건 들고나가면 끝
try	[word] 계정 **account** 사고 싶은 물건 **pick items what they want**
text	업계선 쇼핑 혁명 신호탄 평가
try	[word] 쇼핑 혁명 신호탄 **a signal of shopping revolution**
text	쇼핑은 즐겁지만 계산대 앞에 줄을 선 뒤 일일이 물건을 꺼내 계산을 하는 과정은 지루하기 짝이 없다.
try	[word] 즐겁다 **joy** 줄을 서다 **wait in line**

| **practice** | In Seattle 'Amazon Go' has run in pilot. |
| **mojo** | In Seattle 'Amazon go' is currently piloting the new store. |

| **practice** | ~~With~~ making an account at smartphone, you can go shopping in there. Customers pick what they want items ~~of goods, carry~~ and go, and then all shopping is finished.
[Suggestion] with making → making pick of goods, carry and go → hold and go |
| **mojo** | Making smartphone account, shopping what you want to buy, and then carrying, it simply ends up your shopping.
[tip] ends up 끝난다 |

| **practice** | The businesses estimate it as a signal of shopping revolution. |
| **mojo** | Business circles say it is a signal of shopping revolution.
[tip] business circles 업계에서는 |

| **practice** | Shopping is joyful, but counting process is boring when it comes to pull back items on counter after waiting in long line. |
| **mojo** | Shopping is joyful, yet waiting in a long line in front of counter to compute all the prices is a quite boring process.
[tip] waiting in a long line 긴 줄에 기다리다 to compute all the prices 물건을 꺼내 계산하다 |

<table>
<tr><td>text</td><td>세계 최대 전자상거래 업체인 아마존이 사람은 없고 물건만 있는 '인공지능(AI) 편의점'을 선보인다.</td></tr>
<tr><td>try</td><td></td></tr>
<tr><td></td><td>[word] 최대 전자상거래 업체 biggest e-commerce</td></tr>
<tr><td>text</td><td>오프라인 서점인 '아마존 서점'을 개설한 데 이어 소매점 시장으로 오프라인 영역을 확장시키려는 움직임이다.</td></tr>
<tr><td>try</td><td></td></tr>
<tr><td></td><td>[word] 영역을 확장시키려는 움직임 moves to expand field</td></tr>
<tr><td>text</td><td>아마존은 5일(현지시간) 미국 시애틀에 167m^2(약 50.5평) 규모의 상점 '아마존 고(Amazon Go)'를 오픈했다고 밝혔다.</td></tr>
<tr><td>try</td><td></td></tr>
<tr><td></td><td>[word] 아마존 고 Amazon Go</td></tr>
</table>

practice	The world biggest on-line commerce, Amazon, ~~is shown~~ an AI Store that is stocked products without cashier.

[Suggestion] is shown → showing

mojo

The world biggest e-commerce, Amazon, is demonstrating AI convenient store to sell goods without any cashier.

[tip] is demonstrating AI convenient store 인공지능 편의점을 선보인다

to sell goods without any cashier. 사람은 없이 물건을 파는

---

practice

Following opening off-line bookstore, Amazon bookshop, it moves to expand field into off-line retail shop.

mojo

It is moving to expand off-line boundary into on-line retail market.

[tip] off-line boundary into on-line retail market 오프라인 영역을 온라인 소매시장으로

---

practice

Amazon on December 5th ~~in~~ local time, revealed Amazon Go ~~has~~ opened 167m^2 sized store at Seattle, the U.S.

[tip] revealed Amazon Go has opened → revealed Amazon Go opened

mojo

Amazon, on local time this month 5th, announced that it opened 'Amazon Go' (167m square) in Chicago, according to Amazon.

[tip] on local time this month 5th 현지시간 이달 5일에

아마존 고는 주로 식료품을 판매하는 편의점으로 우선 아마존 직원을 대상으로 시범 운영 한 뒤 내년 초 일반에 공개할 예정이다.

[word] 주로 mainly   식료품 foodstuffs   아마존 직원 its employee
일반에 in the public

practice

It is a kind of food convenience store, first of all they will run targeting Amazon's employees and then it will set to be open ~~in~~ public as early as next year.

[Suggestion] to be open in public as early as next year → to be open to public early next year

mojo

Amazon Go is convenient store mainly selling foodstuffs. It first intends for its employees, and then will be open for the public early next year.

[tip] mainly selling foodstuffs 주로 식료품을 판매하는

intends for its employee 직원을 위한 것이다 **for the public** 일반에

모두가 힘을 모으면, AI 조기에 종식시킬 수 있습니다.

"국민 여러분 지켜주세요."
1. 철새도래지와 축산농가 방문을 최대한 자제
2. 불가피하게 방문한 경우에는 아래사항을 준수
차량 방문 시 소독시설을 통과하여 차량을 소독
도보 방문 시에도 설치된 발판 소독조 반드시 이용
철새의 사체, 배설물 등을 밟거나 접촉하지 않도록 유의
3. AI 발생지역 해외여행 자제
여행지역 가금농장 출입 금지
귀국 시 닭 · 오리고기 반입 금지

text	모두가 힘을 모으면, AI 조기에 종식시킬 수 있습니다.
try	[word] 힘을 모으다 **gather effort**　조류독감 **AI · Avian Influenza**　종식하다 **end**
text	"국민 여러분 지켜주세요."
try	[word] 국민 **public**　여러분 **all of you**

30

Mojo Writing

We can eradicate AI early enough if we make an effort together.

Everybody, please, keep to

1. Restrain from visiting the sites of migratory birds or stock farmers.

2. In case of an unavoidable visit to the places, please observe following matters: In case of vehicle travels, it is required that vehicles be disinfected through facilities of sterilization,
In case of visit by walk, visitors are required to use disinfected foothold, and required not to tread or touch corpse of birds.

3. Restrain from travel abroad if possible, and carrying in chicken or duck meat is not allowed when homecoming.

practice	When we gather our effort ~~up~~, Avian Influenza ~~let cease~~ from spreading. **[Suggestion] up → together let cease → may be stopped**
mojo	**We can eradicate AI early enough if we make an effort together.** **[tip] eradicate** 근절하다 · 전멸시키다 **make an effort together** 함께 노력하다
practice	"Keep following, Korean citizens, please."
mojo	**Everybody, please, keep to** **[tip] please, keep to** 지켜주세요

text	1. 철새도래지와 축산농가 방문을 최대한 자제
try	
	[word] 철새도래지 **bird sanctuary** 자제 **restrain**

text	2. 불가피하게 방문한 경우에는 아래사항을 준수
try	
	[word] 불가피하게 방문 **unavoidable travel** 아래사항 **followings** 준수 **abide by**

text	차량 방문 시 소독시설을 통과하여 차량을 소독
try	
	[word] 차량 방문 **vehicle visit** 소독 **disinfection** 살균 **sterilization**

text	도보 방문 시에도 설치된 발판 소독조 반드시 이용 철새의 사체, 배설물 등을 밟거나 접촉하지 않도록 유의
try	
	[word] 설치된 발판 **installed foothold** 철새의 사체 **corpse of birds**

practice ~~As long as~~ restrain from visiting to the sites of migratory birds or cattle farms.

[Suggestion] as long as restrain → restrain

mojo Restrain from visiting the sites of migratory birds or stock farmers.

[tip] the sites of migratory birds 철새서식처 **stock farmers** 축산농가

---

practice Abiding by next, as it is unavoidable travel.

mojo In case of an unavoidable visit to the places, please observe following matters:

[tip] please observe following matters 아래 사항을 준수하세요

---

practice Disinfect vehicles through facilities of sterilization at the sites.

mojo In case of vehicle travels, it is required that vehicles be disinfected through facilities of sterilization,

[tip] it is required that 필수적이다

throughfacilities of sterilization 살균 시설을 통하여

---

practice Required using set up disinfect foothold at the visiting by walking.

Attention not to step or contact on the corpse birds or its feces.

mojo In case of visit by walk, visitors are required to use disinfected foothold, and required not to tread or touch corpse of birds or its feces.

3. AI 발생지역 해외여행 자제
여행지역 가금농장 출입 금지
귀국 시 닭 · 오리고기 반입 금지

[word] AI 발생지역 **AI origin** 닭 · 오리고기 반입금지 **ban to return with chicken or duck**

Refrain traveling the foreign place of AI origin.

Off places from the poultry farm around traveling course.

Banning return with roosters or ducks back home country.

[Suggestion] refrain → restrain

Restrain from travel abroad if possible, and carrying in chicken or duck meat is not allowed when homecoming.

[tip] Restrain from travel abroad 해외여행 자제 carrying in 반입

✏️

미리 맛 좀 볼까요

올림픽 코스서 씽~

2017년 시즌(2016년 11월~2017년 4월) 오픈을 앞둔
지난 달 초 스키장 관계자가 "희망"이라는 단어를 언급했다.
뜻밖이었다.
"암담하다" "걱정이다" 따위의 어두운 말만 입에 달고 살던
스키장 업계가 오랜만에 희망을 말했기 때문이다.
실제로 침체 일로였던 국내 스키(스노보드 포함) 인구는
지난 시즌 변동의 조짐을 나타냈다.

text	미리 맛 좀 볼까요
try	

[word] 미리 **in advance · beforehand** 맛 **taste**

text	올림픽 코스서 씽~
try	

[word] 올림픽 코스 **the course of Olympic**

31

Mojo Writing

How do you like to taste it beforehand?

We would whiz by the course of Olympic winter sports.

Early in the last month, close to opening the game of the 2017 season (November 2016-April 2017), an official relate to skiing resort mentioned a word 'hope.' It came as unexpected: the skis business had a way with saying words "dismal" and "anxiety." The population of national skis on the way steady decline indeed, including snowboard, showed somewhat of change during last season.

practice	Beforehand, try to know how ~~tastes it is~~. **[Suggestion] howtastes it is → how it tastes it**
mojo	How do you like to taste it beforehand? **[tip] How do you like to** ~할까요
practice	Running by whiz ~~at~~ the course of Olympic. **[Suggestion] at the course of Olympic·on the course of Olympic**
mojo	We would whiz by the course of Olympic winter sports. **[tip] whiz** 쉭 소리와 더불어 빠르게 지나가다

text

2017년 시즌 오픈을 앞둔 지난 달 초 스키장 관계자가 "희망"이라는 단어를 언급했다.

try

[word] 2017년 시즌(2016년11월~2017년 4월) **the game of the 2017 season, November 2016-April 2017,**

text

뜻밖이었다. "암담하다""걱정이다" 따위의 어두운 말만 입에 달고 살던 스키장 업계가 오랜만에 희망을 말했기 때문이다.

try

[word] 뜻밖이다 · 의외다 **unexpected** 암담 **gloomy**

text

실제로 침체 일로였던 국내 스키(스노보드 포함) 인구는 지난 시즌 변동의 조짐을 나타냈다.

try

[word] 실제로 **in fact** 침체 **slump**

practice

Ahead of opening the season in 2017, from November 2016 to April 2017, at the early of last month, an official related to the ski resort mentioned the word of hope.

mojo

Early in the last month, close to opening the game of the 2017 season (November 2016- April 2017), an official relate to skiing resort mentioned a word 'hope.'

[tip] **close to opening** 오픈을 앞두고 **an official relate to skiing resort** 스키장 관계자가

---

practice

It was unexpected it. That's why the ski businesskeeping on saying usually gloomy words, such as dark or worry, told hope in a long time.

mojo

It came as unexpected: the skis businesshad a way with saying words "dismal" and "anxiety."

[tip] **It came as unexpected** 뜻밖이었다

had a way with saying 말을 하는 식이었다

---

practice

In fact, domestic ski population, including snowboard, have been on verge of slump, eventually showed a signal of change in past season.

mojo

The population of national skis on the way steady decline indeed, including snowboard, showed somewhat of change during last season.

[tip] **on the way steady decline indeed** 실제로 침체 일로의 길에 있는

a signal of change 변화의 조짐

버핏 올해 재산 14조 원 늘었다

불룸버그 통신 "트럼프 당선 덕"
부호 1위 빌 게이츠는 11조 원 증가
투자의 귀재 워런 버핏(86) 버크셔해서웨이 최고경영자(CEO)가
올해 세계에서 재산을 가장 많이 불리며 세계 두 번째 부호로 올라섰다고
블룸버그 통신이 11일(현지시간) 보도했다.
이 통신이 집계한 세계 억만장자 상위 500명 자료(9일 기준)에 따르면
버핏은 올해 전 세계 부호 중 가장 많은 117억 달러(13조 7000억 원)의
재산을 늘렸다.
버핏의 재산 증가는 미국 대선에서 도널드 트럼프의 당선 덕이라고
통신은 분석했다.
대선 기간 반 트럼프 의사를 밝혀온 버핏은 역설적이게도
트럼프의 당선 이후 나타난 주가 상승으로 가장 큰 수혜를 받았다.

text	버핏 올해 재산 14조 원 늘었다
try	[word] 버핏 **Buffett** 재산 **property**
text	불룸버그 통신 "트럼프 당선 덕"
try	[word] 불룸버그 통신 **Bloomberg News**

32

Mojo Writing

Buffett increased his fortune by 14 trillion won this year.

Bloomberg said "it is thank to the election of Trump."
As number one billionaire, Bill Gates has increased 11 Trillion won in his fortune.
The investment wizard, Warren Buffett, 86, CEO of Berkshire Hathaway, got his fortune most swollen this year and stood out as the second richest in the world, the Bloomberg said.
According to the world's 500 richest billionaires, published by the media, Buffett increased his wealth the most among the world's richest by accumulating $11.7bln this year. The Bloomberg only analyzes that Trump's election has made a contribution to the increment of his wealth. It may sound ironical, but he has benefitted most from rising in stocks, despite the fact that he was against Trump during his presidential campaign trail.

practice	Buffett has increased his property by ~~about~~ 14trillion won in this year. **[Suggestion] about → some**
mojo	Buff increased his fortune by 14trillion won this year. **[tip] his fortune** 그의 재산
practice	According to Bloomberg News, it was served that ~~Trump elected as~~ the U.S. president. **[Suggestion] Trump elected as → Trump was elected as**
mojo	Bloomberg said "it is thank to the election of Trump." **[tip] it is thank to** 덕 · 덕택

text	부호 1위 빌 게이츠는 11조 원 증가
try	

[word] 빌 게이츠 **Bill Gates**

text	투자의 귀재 워런 버핏(86) 버크셔해서웨이 최고경영자가 올해 세계에서 재산을 가장 많이 불리며 세계 두 번째 부호로 올라섰다고 블룸버그 통신이 11일(현지시간) 보도했다.
try	

[word] 투자의 귀재 · 마법사 **the investment wizard**　버크셔해서웨이 최고 경영자 **CEO of Berkshire Hathaway**

text	이 통신이 집계한 세계 억만장자 상위 500명 자료(9일 기준)에 따르면 버핏은 올해 전 세계 부호 중 가장 많은 117억 달러(13조 7000억 원)의 재산을 늘렸다.
try	

[word] 집계 **tally**　세계 억만장자 상위 500명 **the world's 500richest billionaires**

| **practice** | The richest of the world, Bill Gates, ~~raised~~ ₩11t.

[Suggestion] raised → rose |
| **mojo** | As number one billionaire, Bill Gates has increased 11 Trillion won in his fortune.

[tip] number one billionaire 부호 1위 |

| **practice** | The prodigy of investigation, Warren Buffett, 86, CEO of Berkshire Hathaway, made swell his fortune to the biggest and rose up the second richest over the world in this year, reported date 11 this month local time to Bloomberg News. |
| **mojo** | The investment wizard, Warren Buffett, 86, CEO of Berkshire Hathaway, got his fortune most swollen this year and stood out as the second richest in the world, the Bloomberg said.

[tip] most swollen 가장 많이 불리며 **stood out** 올라섰다 · 두드러졌다 |

| **practice** | According to the Media tallied data with the world top 500 date 9 same month, Buffett increased the biggest gain with $11.7b among the world richest. |
| **mojo** | According to the world's 500 richest billionaires, published by the media, Buffett increased his wealth the most among the world's richest by accumulating $11.7bln this year.

[tip] published by the media 그 통신이 보도한 |

버핏의 재산 증가는 미국 대선에서 도널드 트럼프의 당선 덕이라고 통신은 분석했다.

[word] 미국 대선 **the U.S. President election**

대선 기간 반 트럼프 의사를 밝혀온 버핏은 역설적이게도 트럼프의 당선 이후 나타난 주가 상승으로 가장 큰 수혜를 받았다.

[word] 역설적 **ironical** 수혜 **benefit**

practice

The media observed its growing ~~is~~ contributed to Donald Trump victory in the U.S. President election.

[Suggestion] its growing is contributed to → its growing contributed to

mojo

The Bloomberg only analyzes that Trump's election has made a contribution to the increment of his wealth.

[tip] **The Bloomberg analyzes that** 블룸버그 통신은 분석했다

---

practice

During the campaign, having revealed anti-Trump, Buffett has got biggest benefit ironically by stock gaining after Trump elected.

mojo

It may sound ironical, but he has benefitted most from rising in stocks, despite the fact that he was against Trump during his presidential campaign trail.

[tip] **it may sound ironical** 역설적이게도 **from rising in stocks** 주식 상승으로 **he was against Trump** 그가 반 트럼프 의사를 밝혔다

독일 빵 '슈톨렌' 어떤 맛이길래…

케이크 대신 즐기는 크리스마스 빵

타원형의 투박한 빵 위에 하얀 슈거 파우더가 눈처럼 쌓였다.
독일의 크리스마스 빵 '슈톨렌(stolen)'의 첫 인상이다.
표면이 딱딱한 빵을 칼로 쓱쓱 썰어보니
속을 풍성하게 채운 건과일·견과류가 시선을 사로잡는다.
묵직하게 퍼지는 럼과 과일의 숙성된 향도 코를 간질인다.
모양도, 풍미도 낯선 이 독일 빵이 올 크리스마스엔
'동그란 케이크' 자리를 넘보고 있다.

text	독일 빵 '슈톨렌' 어떤 맛이길래…
try	[word] 독일 빵 슈톨렌 **German bread, Stolen**
text	케이크 대신 즐기는 크리스마스 빵
try	[word] 즐기는 **enjoy · take pleasure in**
text	타원형의 투박한 빵 위에 하얀 슈거 파우더가 눈처럼 쌓였다. 독일의 크리스마스 빵 '슈톨렌(stolen)'의 첫 인상이다.
try	[word] 타원형 **elliptical** 투박한 빵 **coarse bread** 하얀 슈거 파우더 **white sugar powder**

33

What would it be to taste German bread, Stolen, like?

People are fond of the Christmas bread instead of cakes.

On the top of the oval shaped coarse bread, white sugar powder was piled up like snow. It is how the German bread, Stolen, looks first. When the bread of its hard surface is sliced with agility, the dry fruits fully stuffed in its inside come into sight at a first glance. The rum's smell hanging in the air and matured fruits aroma make noses feels insatiable. It's look and flavor are strange, but it covets the seats of rounded cake during upcoming Christmas season.

practice	What Stolen, German bread, is taste like?
mojo	**What would it be to taste German bread, Stolen, like?**
	[tip] to taste like 어떤 맛
practice	It is a kind of bread getting pleasure in Christmas season ~~rather than~~ cake. **[Suggestion] rather than → instead of**
mojo	**People are fond of the Christmas bread instead of cakes.** **[tip] be fond of** 좋아하다
practice	The top of the rustic oval shaped bread was powered sugar like snowing. It was first impressed by Stolen in Christmas season.
mojo	**On the top of the oval shaped coarse bread, white sugar powder was piled up like snow.** **[tip] was piled up like snow** 눈처럼 쌓였다

<table>
<tr><td>text</td><td>표면이 딱딱한 빵을 칼로 쓱쓱 썰어보니 속을 풍성하게 채운 건과일·견과류가 시선을 사로잡는다.</td></tr>
<tr><td>try</td><td></td></tr>
</table>

[word] 표면 **surface**　건과일　견과류 **dried fruits and nuts**

<table>
<tr><td>text</td><td>묵직하게 퍼지는 럼과 과일의 숙성된 향도 코를 간질인다.</td></tr>
<tr><td>try</td><td></td></tr>
</table>

[word] 묵직하다 **heavy**　럼 **rum**　숙성된 향·익은 향 **ripen fruits flavor**

<table>
<tr><td>text</td><td>모양도, 풍미도 낯선 이 독일 빵이 올 크리스마스엔 '동그란 케이크' 자리를 넘보고 있다.</td></tr>
<tr><td>try</td><td></td></tr>
</table>

[word] 모양 **shape**　풍미 **flavor**　낯선 **strange**

practice

When the harden crust of Stolen is cut easily with knife, fully mixed dried fruits and nuts is caught your sight.

mojo

It is how the German bread, Stolen, looks first. When the bread of its hard surface is sliced with agility, the dry fruits fully stuffed in its inside come into sight at a first glance.

[tip] **it is how stolen looks first** 첫째로 눈에 보인다 · 시선을 사로 잡는다

hard surface is sliced with agility 딱딱한 빵은 민첩하게 쓱쓱 썰리다

the dry fruits fully stuffed in its inside 풍성하게 채운 견과류들

practice

And then both gravely spreading rum smell and ripening fruits flavor spur your olfactory cell.

mojo

The rum's smell hanging in the air and matured fruits aroma make noses feels insatiable.

[tip] **hanging in the air** 공중에 퍼지다 **matured fruits aroma** 숙성된 과일 향 **noses feels insatiable** 코가 만족할 줄 모르는 느낌이다 · 탐욕스러움을 느끼다

practice

Somewhat odd shaped and flavored the German Bread has dominated on the site of rounded cakes ~~in this Christmas~~.

[Suggestion] **inthis Christmas → in this Christmas season**

mojo

Its look and flavor are strange, but it covets the seats of rounded cake during upcoming Christmas season.

[tip] **its look and flavor are strange** 모양도, 풍미도 낯선 **it covets the seats of rounded cake** 동그란 케이크 자리를 넘보고 있다

양고기 바람 타고 중국 술 판매 날개

중국 술을 찾는 수요가 늘어나고 있다.
이마트에 따르면 지난해 11월 대비 올 11월 중국 바이주(백주) 매출은
92.5% 늘었다.
사케(88.8%)보다 신장 폭이 크고
위스키(10.6%)와는 상대가 되지 않을 정도다.
중국 술의 인기 배경에는 양고기가 있다고 유통업체들은 보고 있다.
해외 여행이나 유학을 통해 접한 양꼬치나 양갈비 같은
중국식 양고기 요리를 국내에서 먹으려는 수요가 늘어
중국 술을 곁들이려는 경우가 증가했다는 것이다.

text	양고기 바람 타고 중국 술 판매 날개
try	[word] 양고기 **mutton**　바람 타고 · 유행 타고 **vogue**　중국 술 판매 **Chinese wine sale**
text	중국 술을 찾는 수요가 늘어나고 있다.
try	[word] 중국 술을 찾는 수요 **the demand of the Chinese wine**

34

Mojo Writing

Chinese wine sale sells like hot cakes in vogue of mutton.

The demand of the Chinese wine is ever growing. According to e-mart, the sale growth of the Chinese white 'Bai' wine increased by 92.5% in the November of this year compared to the same November of last year. It's sales growth is bigger the Japanese 'Sake' (88.8%), especially it is more than a match for whisky (10.6%). Distribution industry sees the popularity of the Chinese wine as the mutton behind. It means that, with experiencing Chinese dishes of mutton skewer and ribs during abroad traveling or study, they would increasingly eat them with Chinese wine in the domestic country.

practice	Chinese wine sale is flying high along with a fad of mutton.
mojo	**Chinese wine sale sells like hot cakes in vogue of mutton.**
	[tip] sale sells like hot cakes 날개 돋친 듯이 팔린다

practice	The demand of Chinese wine is growing.
mojo	**The demand of the Chinese wine is ever growing**
	[tip] is ever growing 지금까지 늘어나고 있다

<table>
<tr><td>text</td><td>이마트에 따르면 지난해 11월 대비 올 11월 중국 바이주(백주) 매출은 92.5%
늘었다.</td></tr>
<tr><td>try</td><td></td></tr>
<tr><td></td><td>[word] 이마트 e-mart 대비 compare to 중국 바이주(백주) the Chinese white 'Bai' wine 매출 the sale growth</td></tr>
<tr><td>text</td><td>사케(88.8%)보다 신장 폭이 크고 위스키(10.6%)와는 상대가 되지 않을
정도다.</td></tr>
<tr><td>try</td><td></td></tr>
<tr><td></td><td>[word] 신장 폭 sale growth 위스키와</td></tr>
<tr><td>text</td><td>중국 술의 인기 배경에는 양고기가 있다고 유통업체들은 보고 있다</td></tr>
<tr><td>try</td><td></td></tr>
<tr><td></td><td>[word] 중국 술의 인기 the popularity of the Chinese wine
유통업체 distribution industry</td></tr>
</table>

practice   According to e-mart data, Chinese white wine sale has increased 92.5% this November compare to same month of previous year.

mojo   According to e-mart, the sale growth of the Chinese white 'Bai' wine increased by 92.5% in the November of this year compared to the same November of last year.

[tip] **In the November of this year compared to the same November of last year** 지난해 11월 대비 올 11월

---

practice   It is not only higher growing than 88.8% Sake, but also nothing matches with 10.6% whiskey.

mojo   It's sales growth is bigger than the Japanese 'Sake' (88.8%), especially it is more than a match for whisky (10.6%).

[tip] **a match for whisky** 위스키에 상대하다

---

practice   Retailers see the whim of Chinese wine as mutton behind.

mojo   Distribution industry sees the popularity of the Chinese wine as the mutton behind.

[tip] **as the mutton behind** 양고기가 배경인 것으로

해외 여행이나 유학을 통해 접한 양꼬치나 양갈비 같은 중국식 양고기 요리를
국내에서 먹으려는 수요가 늘어 중국 술을 곁들이려는 경우가 증가했다는 것이다

[word] 양꼬치 mutton skewer   양갈비 mutton rib

practice

With being close to lamb skewer or chops in traveling or studying abroad, so people demand more Chinese style lamb dishes that they want more put adding with Chinese wine in their dinner.

[Suggestion] inthis Christmas → in this Christmas season

mojo

It means that, with experiencing Chinese dishes of mutton skewer and ribs during abroad traveling or study, they would increasingly eat them with Chinese wine in the domestic country.

[tip] during abroad traveling or study 해외 여행이나 유학을 통해

text	개인이 행복한 사회
try	[word] 개인 **individual**
text	'야간의 주간화, 휴일의 평일화'
try	[word] 야간 **night** 주간 **day time** 평일 **weekday**
text	'가정 초토화, 라면의 상식화'
try	[word] 가정 **family** 초토화 **waste**

35

Mojo Writing

The society of which individual is happy.

The night turns out to be daytime. Holiday feels like weekday.
Family is laid waste, the ramen feeds people.
It is the business guideline of the Blue House, which the last
former chief of civil affair left behind in his note.There was a mark
signifying that the words came from chief of secretary, containing
some added words that the Blue house is a place to eat honor at, of
no pleasure and only royal devotion required.
What is necessary in Korean society instead is the respect of
private territory, once we make a clear distinction between public
and private matters, and respect the mutual privates sector, we can
only do our best for public area.

practice	The Society of individual being happy
mojo	**The society of which individual is happy.**
	[tip] of which individual is happy 그 안의 개인이 행복한

practice	'The night turns to be day time, holyday changes to business day.'
mojo	**The night turns out to be daytime. Holiday feels like weekday.**
	[tip] turn out 되다 **feel like weekday** 주간처럼 느끼다

practice	'Family makes to lay it waste, Ramen feeds usual.'
mojo	**Family is laid waste, the ramen feeds people.**
	[tip] be laid waste 초토화 되다 **feed people** 사람을 먹이다

text	지난 8월 사망한 김영한 전 청와대 민정수석이 남긴 수첩에 적힌 청와대의 업무지침이다.
try	

[word] 사망 demise   전 민정수석 **former chief of civil affair**   업무지침 **business guideline**

---

text	그것은 비서실장의 말임을 뜻하는 표시가 있었다. (청와대는) 명예를 먹는 곳이며 어떤 즐거움도 없고 모든 것을 바쳐 헌신해야 한다는 내용도 덧붙여져 있다.
try	

[word] 비서실장 **chief of secretary**   표시 **a mark**   명예 **honor**   즐거움 **joy**
헌신 **devotion**   덧붙이다 **add**

---

text	한국 사회에 있어서 필요한 것은 오히려 사적인 영역의 존중이다. 공과 사를 명확히 구분하고 사적인 부분을 존중할 때 비로소 공적인 부분에서도 최선을 다할 수 있는 것이다.
try	

[word] 사적인 영역 **private territory**   존중 **respect**   공과 사 **public and
private matters**   구분 **distinction**

practice

It was written the guideline of Blue House in a note which has left the former chief of civil affair demised last August.

mojo

It is the business guideline of the Blue House, which the last former chief of civil affair left behind in his note.

[tip] **the last former chief of civil affair** 작고한 전 민정수석

left behind in his note 남긴 수첩에

---

practice

There was a mark of the chief of secretary's mention, adding Blue House is a place where is keeping honor and ready for nix of joy, and then dedicates sacrifice to everything.

[Suggestion] **for nix of joy** 즐거움이 없는

mojo

There was a mark signifying that the words came from the chief of secretary, containing some added words that the Blue house is a place to eat honor at, of no pleasure and only royal devotion required.

[tip] **a mark signifying** 뜻하는 표시 **a place to eat honor at** 명예를 먹는 장소

no pleasure 즐거움도 없고 **only royal devotion required** 충성만을 헌신해야 한다

---

practice

~~Rather than~~ what needs in Korean society is put value to privacy. If makes clear between public jobs and private, and esteems for individual part, finally people is able to do their best in public area.

[Suggestion] **Rather than what needs → What needs**

mojo

What is necessary in Korean society instead is the respect of private territory, once we make a clear distinction between public and private matters, and respect the mutual privates sector, we can only do our best for public area.

[tip] **what is necessary** 필요한 것은 **the respect of private territory** 사적인 영역의 존중 **the mutual privates sector** 상호 사적인 부분

북한, 석탄수출 막히자 '해삼 장사'

품질 좋아 중국에서 고가에 팔려
전복 등 연체동물 북·중 무역 2위
대북 광물제재에 수출 다변화 전략

북한의 외화 수입원으로 연체동물이 급부상했다.
중국 해관(세관)이 발표한
북·중간 무역거래 통계를 분석한 결과
연체동물은 지난 6월부터 매달 석탄에 이어
수출액이 둘째로 많은 품목으로 집계됐다.
그동안 북한의 대표적 수출품으로 알려진
봉제 의류나 기타 농산품보다도
연체동물 수출로 벌어들인 외화가 더 많다는 얘기다.
이는 중국인들이 고급 식재료로 선호하는
해삼·전복·성게·오징어 등
해산물의 북한산 수입이 최근 급증한 데 따른 것으로 풀이된다.

text	북한, 석탄수출 막히자 '해삼 장사'
try	

[word] 석탄수출 coal export 해삼 sea slug

36

North Korea has embarked on selling sea slug as its coal export was blocked.

Because of high quality of the sea slug from North Korea, it sells at very high price in China.
The sea slug and mollusk are placed in second for the trade between North Korea and China.
It is seen as the strategy for diversified approach of export in its response to sanctions of coal against North Korea.

The mollusk has emerged as one of its new source of foreign money. The analysis of the statistics of mutual trade between North Korea and China shows that the export of mollusk continues to come as second place every month following the coal ever since last June. The North Korea has earned more foreign money by exporting the mollusk than clothing and other agricultural goods, which are known as typical export goods of North Korea. This situation explains that Chinese are recently increasing to import their favorite seafood from North Korea, such as sea slug, abalone, sea urchin and squid.

practice	North Korea came to sell sea slugs, when its coal exporting was blocked.
mojo	North Korea has embarked on selling sea slug as its coal export was blocked.

[tip] **has embarked** 시작하다 **on selling sea slug** 해삼장사

was blocked 막혔다

text	전복 등 연체동물 북·중 무역 2위
try	[word] 연체동물 mollusk 북·중 무역 the trade between North Korea and China
text	품질 좋아 중국에서 고가에 팔려
try	[word] 품질 좋아 high quality 고가 high price
text	대북 광물제재에 수출 다변화 전략
try	[word] 광물제재 sanctions of coal 다변화 diversify 전략 strategy
text	북한의 외화 수입원으로 연체동물이 급부상했다.
try	[word] 외화 foreign money 수입원 source of income 급부상 emerge

practice The sea slugs and mollusks place the second post in North Korea-China trade.

mojo The sea slug and mollusk are placed in second for the trade between North Korea and China.

[tip] **are placed in second** 2위에 놓이다

practice The sea food sells pricy in China because of their high quality.

mojo Because of high quality of the sea slug from North Korea, it sells at very high price in China.

[tip] **it sells at very high price** 고가에 팔리다

practice They are diversifying in their exportation against sanctions of North Korea coals.

mojo It is seen as the strategy for diversified approach of export in its response to sanctions of coal against North Korea.

[tip] **response to sanctions of coal against North Korea** 대북 광물제재에 **diversified approach of export** 수출 다변화

practice The mollusks have emerged quickly as foreign money sources of North Korea.

mojo The mollusk has emerged as one of its new source of foreign money.

[tip] **has emerged as one** 하나로 급부상했다

text	중국 해관(세관)이 발표한 북 · 중간 무역거래 통계를 분석한 결과 연체동물은 지난 6월부터 매달 석탄에 이어 수출액이 둘째로 많은 품목으로 집계됐다.
try	
	[word] 북 · 중간 무역거래 통계 **the statistics of mutual trade between North Korea and China** 품목 **item**
text	그동안 북한의 대표적 수출품으로 알려진 봉제 의류나 기타 농산품보다도 연체동물 수출로 벌어들인 외화가 더 많다는 얘기다.
try	
	[word] 대표적 수출품 **typical export goods** 봉제 의류 **clothing** 기타 농산품 **other agricultural goods**
text	이는 중국인들이 고급 식재료로 선호하는 해삼 · 전복 · 성게 · 오징어 등 해산물의 북한산 수입이 최근 급증한 데 따른 것으로 풀이된다.
try	
	[word] 선호 **their favorite** 고급 식재료 **high quality foodstuff** 풀이된다 **explain** 해삼 · 전복 · 성게 · 오징어 **sea slug, abalone, sea urchin and squid**

practice	According to analyzed result ~~from~~ the Statistic of North Korea-China trade reported, the sea food found to the second item tracing the amount of coal each month from last June.
	[Suggestion] resultfrom the Statistic of → result by the Statistic of
mojo	The analysis of the statistics of mutual trade between North Korea and China shows that the export of mollusk continues to come as second place every month following the coal ever since last June.
	[tip] continues to come as second place 둘째 순위로 계속되다
	following the coal 석탄에 이어

practice	It seems that mollusks have earned more foreign money than to be known as NK leading export's items like clothing and other agricultural goods.
mojo	The North Korea has earned more foreign money by exporting the mollusk than clothing and other agricultural goods, which are known as typical export goods of North Korea.
	[tip] Has earned more foreign money 더 많은 외화를 벌다

practice	The situation is described that China has surged to import high quality NK seafood such as sea slug, abalone, sea urchin, squid and all that.
mojo	This situation explains that Chinese are recently increasing to import their favorite seafood from North Korea, such as sea slug, abalone, sea urchin and squid.
	[tip] this situation explains that 상황은 이렇게 풀이된다

✎

월가 경영자 요직 점령, 이번에도 '거버먼트삭스'(골드만삭스 출신 많은 정부)

미국 도널드 트럼프 내각의 경제 라인은
'월가의 부유한 경영자'로 요약된다.
특히 미국 최대 투자은행인 골드만삭스 출신이 줄줄이 요직을 차지했다.
골드만삭스는 '거버먼트삭스(Government+Sachs: 골드만정부) 라는
별칭을 다시 한번 입증했다.
이들은 공직 경험은 없지만 현장 실무 경험은 풍부한 이들이다.

text	월가 경영자 요직 점령, 이번에도 '거버먼트삭스'(골드만삭스 출신 많은 정부)
try	[word] 월가 경영자 Wall Street CEOs 요직 key position 점령 occupy 거버먼트삭스 GovernmentSachs
text	미국 도널드 트럼프 내각의 경제 라인은 '월가의 부유한 경영자'로 요약된다. 특히 미국 최대 투자은행인 골드만삭스 출신이 줄줄이 요직을 차지했다.'
try	[word] 도널드 트럼프 내각의 경제 라인 Trump's administration economic line 최대 투자은행인 골드만삭스 Goldman Sacks, U.S. largest investment bank

37

Mojo Writing

Wall Street CEOs have occupied key positions, so call 'GovenmentSachs'-Trump's administration with ever more people from 'Goldman Sacks.'

The incoming Trump's administration economic line is unusally epitomized as rich CEOs of the Wall Street Businessmen from 'Goldman Sacks,' U.S. largest investment bank, have been appointed to key posts all rows in his administration. The Goldman Sacks has demonstrated once again its nickname as GovenmentSacks. The new appointees have no administrative experience in public service, but men of well-learned business handle.

practice	With Wall Street's CEOs have occupied key positions, coming government also makes a GovernmentSachs.
mojo	Wall Street CEOs have occupied key positions, so call 'GovenmentSachs'-Trump's administration with ever more people from 'Goldman Sacks.' [tip] **With ever more people** 지금까지 더 많은 사람들로
practice	The financial cabinet line of the U.S. for Donald Trump can abstract to wealthiest CEOs from Wall Street. Especially, people come from Goldman Sachs, the U.S. largest investor, took up main seats.
mojo	The incoming Trump's administration economic line is usually epitomized as rich CEOs of the Wall Street Businessmen from 'Goldman Sacks,' U.S. largest investment bank, have been appointed to key posts all rows in his administration. [tip] **is epitomized as rich CEOs** 부유한 경영자로 요약되다 **have been appointed to key posts** 요직에 임명되다

| **text** | 골드만삭스는 '거버먼트삭스(Government+Sachs: 골드만정부') 라는 별칭을 다시 한번 입증했다. |
| **try** | |

[word] 별칭 **nickname**　입증하다 **prove**

| **text** | 이들은 공직 경험은 없지만 현장 실무 경험은 풍부한 이들이다. |
| **try** | |

[word] 공직 **civil service**　경험 **experience**　실무 **business handle**

practice

The Goldman Sachs proved clear their nickname as GovernmentSachs once again.

mojo

The Goldman Sacks has demonstrated once again its nickname as GovenmentSacks.

[tip] **has demonstrated once again** 다시 한번 입증하다 · 나타내다

---

practice

They have yet to experience in public service, but have affluent of financial handles.

mojo

The new appointees have no administrative experience in public service, but men of well-learned business handle.

[tip] **have no administrative experience** 공직 경험은 없다 **well-learned business handle** 실무 경험이 풍부한

**연말 파티룩, 품격 있거나 캐주얼 하거나
모임에 어울리는 스타일링법**

어김없이 연말이 다가왔다.
어수선한 분위기지만 가족과 친구, 동료와
한 해를 마무리하는 자리는 하나 둘쯤 있게 마련이다.
연말 모임이 잡히면 '뭘 입고 갈까' 하는 고민이 앞선다.
가끔 보는 사이라면 잘 사는 모습을 보여주고 싶고,
자주 보는 사이라면 모처럼
연말 기분을 내는 옷차림을 보여주고 싶기 때문이다.
참석자들에게 일정한 복장을 갖출 것을 요구하는
'드레스 코드'가 있는 경우는 고민이 더욱 깊어진다.

text	연말 파티룩, 품격 있거나 캐주얼 하거나 모임에 어울리는 스타일링법
try	
	[word] 연말 year-end 파티룩 **wear for party** 품격 **decent** 캐주얼 **casual**
text	어김없이 연말이 다가왔다.
try	
	[word] 어김 없다 **never fails**

38

Mojo Writing

Attire for the year-end party, whether it looks elegant or casual, should be the style to go well with the meeting.

The year-end is never missing. Things are busy around us already. Yet we may arrange one or two occasions to sit with members of our family, friends or colleagues, spending time of the year-end with them.

Once the meeting of the year-end is scheduled, we wonder which one of our clothes we wear to the meeting.

If they are ones you meet from time to time, it is no doubt you would make yourself look well-off.

Otherwise, you may show them how appealing you are to make them feel on a whim of the end of year.

If some specific dress code is required for participants, it's way of getting them more upset.

practice	Looking of where is in the year-end party is decent attired or clothed casual. The way of matched styling in a meeting
mojo	**Attire for the year-end party, whether it looks elegant or casual, should be the style to go well with the meeting.**

[tip] **attire for the year-end party** 연말 파티 의상 **whether it looks elegant or casual** 품격 있거나 캐주얼 하거나 **the style to go well with the meeting** 모임에 어울리는 스타일

practice	The end of year never fails to around the corner.
mojo	**The year-end is never missing.**

[tip] **is never missing** 놓치지 않다

text

어수선한 분위기지만 가족과 친구, 동료와 한 해를 마무리하는 자리는
하나 둘쯤 있게 마련이다.

try

[word] 어수선한 분위기 **disarranged mood** 동료 **college**
자리 · 모임 **meeting · gathering**

---

text

연말 모임이 잡히면 '뭘 입고 갈까' 하는 고민이 앞선다.

try

[word] 연말 모임 **a meeting of the year-end** 고민 **wonder**

---

text

가끔 보는 사이라면 잘 사는 모습을 보여주고 싶고, 자주 보는 사이라면 모처럼
연말 기분을 내는 옷차림을 보여주고 싶기 때문이다.

try

[word] 가끔 **from time to time** 자주 **regularly**
연말 기분을 내는 옷차림 **a whim of the end of year**

practice

Korean society is in upset situation, but many people will arrange one or two seats for year-ending with family, friends and colleges.

mojo

[tip] **things are busy around us** 주위가 바쁘다 **may arrange one or two occasions** 하나 둘쯤 있게 마련일 것이다

---

practice

Once ~~meeting set~~, how dress up for the party gets mind in advance.

[Suggestion] **once meeting set → once meeting is set**

mojo

[tip] **once a meeting is scheduled** 모임이 잡히면 **our clothes we wear to the meeting** 입고 갈 옷

---

practice

While the relations ~~among~~ is once in a while, you would look to wealthy, if it is close relations, so that you want to show dressing of the year-end mood enough.

[Suggestion] **while the relations among is → while the relations is**

mojo

[tip] **It is no doubt you would make yourself look well-off** 잘 사는 모습을 보여주고 싶다 **you may show them how appealing you** 보여주고 싶을지도 모른다

참석자들에게 일정한 복장을 갖출 것을 요구하는 '드레스 코드'가 있는 경우는 고민이 더욱 깊어진다.

[word] 참석자 **participant** 일정한 복장 **specific dress code**
요구하는 **is required**

In the case of having a dress code, asking for fixed attire for attendee, you fall in nervous further with it.

If some specific dress code is required for participants, it's way of getting them more upset.

[tip] **it's way of getting more upset** 고민이더욱 깊어진다

"사드는 차기 정권 넘기고, 개성공단 즉각 재개해야"

도올이 묻고 문재인이 답하다
정세의 급격한 변화가 대선주자로서 문재인의 위상을 중후하게
만들고 있는 것은 부정할 수 없는 사실이다.
이럴 때일수록 그의 발언과 그 배면에 깔린 그의 의도를
정확하게 짚어 보는 것은 국민들이 이 시대를 진단하고
바른 평가를 내리는 데 도움을 주리라 믿는다.
문재인은 조류독감 농가의 실태를 알아보기 위해 농촌으로 떠난다고 했다.
도올은 14일 그를 마포의 어느 카페에서 아침 일찍 만났다.

text	"사드는 차기 정권 넘기고, 개성공단 즉각 재개해야"
try	

[word] 사드 · 고고도지역방어체계 **Terminal High Altitude Area Defense** 차기 정권 **the next administration** 개성공단 **the Kaesung Industrial Complex** 재개 **resume**

text	도올이 묻고 문재인이 답하다
try	

[word] 도올 **Dole** 문재인 **Moon Jaein**

39

Mojo Writing

"The THAAD issue should be handed over to the next administration, and the kaesung Industrial Complex must be resumed immediately."

Dole asked and Moon Jae-in gave the answer to it.

It is no longer deniable that an unexpected change has brought the presumed presidential runner to a political heavy-weight of stature.

Whatever it may be, it is still more important to weigh his rhetoric and every nuance in his voice for public to read the times and judge it right.

Moon said he was going down to the rural to look at the actual conditions of avian influenza.

Dole met him early morning on this month 14th at one of cafes of Mapo district.

practice	"The THAAD issue ~~is~~ handed over next administration, the inter-Korean Industrial Complex has must resume right away." **[Suggestion] the THAAD issue is handed over → the THAAD issue should be handed over**
mojo	**"The THAAD issue should be handed over to the next administration, and the Kaesung Industrial Complex must be resumed immediately."** **[tip] should be handed over to the next administration** 차기 정권에 넘겨야만 한다 **must be resumed** 재개해야 한다
practice	Dole asks and Mr. Moon answers.
mojo	Dole asked and Moon Jaein gave the answer to it. **[tip] gave the answer to it** 그것에 대답하다

<table>
<tr><td>text</td><td>정세의 급격한 변화가 대선주자로서 문재인의 위상을 중후하게 만들고 있는 것은 부정할 수 없는 사실이다.</td></tr>
<tr><td>try</td><td></td></tr>
</table>

[word] 정세 · 상황 **situation** 대선주자 **presidential runner** 위상 **stature**
중후하다 **grave**

<table>
<tr><td>text</td><td>이럴 때일수록 그의 발언과 그 배면에 깔린 그의 의도를 정확하게 짚어 보는 것은 국민들이 이 시대를 진단하고 바른 평가를 내리는 데 도움을 주리라 믿는다.</td></tr>
<tr><td>try</td><td></td></tr>
</table>

[word] 발언 **comment** 의도 **intention**   짚어보다 **count on** 진단 **weigh**
평가 **judge**

<table>
<tr><td>text</td><td>문재인은 조류독감 농가의 실태를 알아보기 위해 농촌으로 떠난다고 했다.</td></tr>
<tr><td>try</td><td></td></tr>
</table>

[word] 조류독감 **Avian Influenza** 농가의 실태 **actual conditionsof farm**

practice	It ~~fails to~~ deniable fact that this swift circumstance makes gravity to the status of Mr. Moon as presidential runner. **[Suggestion] it fails to → it doesn't to be**
mojo	**It is no longer deniable that an unexpected change has brought the presumed presidential runner to a political heavy-weight of stature.** **[tip] It is no longer deniable** 더 이상 부정할 수 없다 **the presumed presidential runner** 대선주자로 짐작되는

practice	In this time, accurate touching what is his mention and intention behind believes to help for people to assess rightly.
mojo	**Whatever it may be, it is still more important to weigh his rhetoric and every nuance in his voice for public to read the times and judge it right.** **[tip] whatever it may be** 그것이 무엇이든 **to weigh his rhetoric and every nuance in his voice** 그의 발언과 그 배면에 깔린 의도를 정확하게 짚어보다 **judge it right** 바른 평가를 내리다

practice	Mr. Moon said he would ~~leave to~~ farm village for looking into the actual condition of avian influenza. **[Suggestion] he would leave to → he would leave for**
mojo	**Moon said he was going down to the rural to look at the actual conditions of avian influenza.** **[tip] be going down to the rural** 농촌으로 내려가다 **to look at the actual condition** 실제상황을 알아보기 위해

도올은 14일 그를 마포의 어느 카페에서 아침 일찍 만났다.

[word] 마포의 어느 카페에서 **at one of café of Mapo district**

Dole met him on 14 of this month early morning in one of café of Mapo district.

Dole met him early morning on this month 14th at one of cafes of Mapo district.

[tip] **early morning on this month 14th** 14일 아침 일찍

에너지 음료 '야(YA)' 카페인 과잉 한 캔 마셔도 하루 권고량 넘어

15일 한국소비자원이 20개 에너지 음료의 카페인 함유량을
조사한 결과에 따르면 삼성제약의 '야(YA)'는 162mg의 카페인을 함유했다.
이는 캔커피(74mg)나 커피믹스(69mg)의 두 배가 넘는 양이다.
청소년(50kg)이 이 음료를 한 캔 마시면
하루 최대 카페인 섭취권고량(125mg)의 130%에 이르는
카페인을 섭취하게 된다.

text	"사드에너지 음료 '야(YA)' 카페인 과잉 한 캔 마셔도 하루 권고량 넘어
try	[word] 에너지 음료 '야(YA)' **energizing beverage Ya** 카페인 과잉 한 캔 **a caffeine excessive can** 하루 권고량 **the daily recommendation**
text	15일 한국소비자원이 20개 에너지 음료의 카페인 함유량을 조사한 결과에 따르면 삼성제약의 '야(YA)'는 162mg의 카페인을 함유했다.
try	[word] 도올 **Dole** 문재인 **Moon Jaein**

40

Mojo Writing

Drinking a caffeine excessive can of energizing beverage Ya exceeds its amount of the daily recommendation.

According to findings of 20 canned energizing beverages made by Korea Consumer Protection Board on this month 15th, the Ya of Samsung Pharmaceutical contains caffeine of 162mg in it. It holds amount of caffeine two times as much as those of canned coffee 74mg and the coffee mix 69mg.
If a teenager, 50kg, drinks one can of the beverage, he may have intake of caffeine, 130% more than daily recommended 125mg.

practice	So the energizer beverage, Ya, is contained excessive amount of caffeine, that even though one can drinking is more than the daily recommendation.
mojo	**Drinking a caffeine excessive can of energizing beverage Ya exceeds its amount of the daily recommendation.** [tip] **drinking a caffeine excessive can of energizing beverage exceeds** 카페인 과잉 음료를 한 캔만 마셔도 초과한다
practice	According to findings of caffeine contamination for 20 canned energizer by Korea Consumer Protection Board in this month 15th, Ya by Samsung Pharmacist was included 162mg caffeine.
mojo	**According to findings of 20 canned energizing beverages made by Korea Consumer Protection Board on this month 15th, the Ya of Samsung Pharmaceutical contains caffeine of 162mg in it.** [tip] **The Ya of Samsung Pharmaceutical contains** 삼성제약의 '야'는 포함한다

text

이는 캔커피(74mg)나 커피믹스(69mg)의 두 배가 넘는 양이다.

try

[word] 정캔커피 **canned coffee beverage** 커피믹스 **the coffee mix**

---

text

청소년(50kg)이 이 음료를 한 캔 마시면 하루 최대 카페인 섭취권고량 (125mg)의 130%에 이르는 카페인을 섭취하게 된다.

try

[word] 청소년 **teenage** 카페인 섭취 **caffeine intake**

<table>
<tr><td>practice</td><td>

It shows more than ~~twice of~~ 74mg of canned coffee beverage or 69mg of mixed powder instant coffee.

[Suggestion] more than twice of → more than two times as much as

</td></tr>
<tr><td>mojo</td><td>

It holds amount of caffeine more than two times as much as those of canned coffee 74mg and the coffee mix 69mg.

[tip] it holds amount of caffeine more than two times 두배가 넘는 양이 들어있다

</td></tr>
</table>

<table>
<tr><td>practice</td><td>

When average teenage, 50mg, drinks one Ya, it leads caffeine intake of 130% of daily recommendation, 125mg.

</td></tr>
<tr><td>mojo</td><td>

If a teenager, 50mg, drinks one can of the beverage, he may have intake of caffeine, 130% more than daily recommended 125mg.

[tip] he may have intake of caffeine 카페인을 섭취하게 되는 것이다

</td></tr>
</table>

‘금리 방아쇠’ 당긴 미국… 세계 달러 끌어당긴다

글로벌 자금 대격변 예고하는 ‘쌍권총’ 옐런 · 트럼프
연준, 내년 3번 더 인상 땐 신흥국 자금 ‘썰물’ 가능성
‘제조업 본국 회귀 정책’에 기업들 투자 미국으로 선회
금 등 안전자산보다 구리 · 니켈 등이 내년 강세 보일 듯
방아쇠는 당겨졌다.
총구는 전세계에 흩뿌려진 미국 달러를 향하고 있다.
미국이 의도했는지 아닌지는 중요하지 않다.
어쨌든 미국은 국제경제의 커다란 흐름을 바꿀 수 있는 힘이 있다.

text	‘금리 방아쇠’ 당긴 미국… 세계 달러 끌어당긴다
try	

[word] 금리 방아쇠 **the trigger of interest rate** 끌어당기다 **pull · draw**

41

Mojo Writing

The US pull of the trigger and global dollars.

With Janet Yellen-Trump as twin guns foretelling global financial upheaval, the financial market of the emerging countries gets possibly chilly, once US Federal Reserve Board raises interest rate 3 times more in the next year.
Ever since Trump's policy of calling U.S. manufacturing industries back, the industries are turning their investments to the U.S.
Instead of gold or safe assets, copper or nickel will likely be bullish in upcoming next year.
The trigger has been pulled, pointing to the U.S. dollars scattered across the world. It makes no matter whether the U.S. intends to do it or not.
Whatever it may be, the U.S. has the power to change the big track of global economy.

practice	~~'The triggered rate' by the U.S~~. draws dollar from around the world. [Suggestion] the triggered rate by the US → the US pulling of the trigger
mojo	**The US pull of the trigger and global dollars.** [tip] **pull of the trigger** 방아쇠를 당기다 **global dollars** 세계 달러

text	글로벌 자금 대격변 예고하는 '쌍권총' 옐런 · 트럼프 연준, 내년 3번 더 인상 땐 신흥국 자금 '썰물' 가능성
try	
	[word] 자금 대격변 **global financial upheaval** 예고하다 **forecast** 쌍권총 **twin guns** 연준 · 연방준비이사회 · **FED: Federal Reserve** 신흥국 **the emerging countries**
text	'제조업 본국 회귀 정책'에 기업들 투자 미국으로 선회
try	
	[word] 제조업 **manufacture** 본국회귀정책 **the policy of calling U.S.** **manufacturing industries back**
text	금 등 안전자산보다 구리 · 니켈 등이 내년 강세 보일 듯
try	
	[word] 금 등 안전자산 **gold and safe assets** 구리 · 니켈 **copper or nickel**

practice

Janet Yellen and Trump like twin guns, warn to huge upheaval of global fund. When the Federal Reserve raises the rate three times, the money ~~in~~ emerging countries will be possible ~~an ebb tide~~.

[Suggestion] the money in emerging countries → the money from the emerging countries will be possible an ebb tide → will be possible flowing away

mojo

With Janet Yellen-Trump as twin guns foretelling global financial upheaval, the financial market of the emerging countries getspossibly chilly once US Federal Reserve Board raises interest rate 3 times more in the next year.

[tip] raise interest rate three times more 세 번 더 금리를 인상하다

---

practice

The policy of returning home for manufactures ~~makes to~~ turn their investment into the U.S.

[Suggestion] makes to turn → help turn

mojo

Ever since Trump's policy of calling U.S. manufacturing industries back, the industries are turning their investments to the U.S.

[tip] the industries are turning their investments to the u.s. 기업들이 투자를 미국으로 선회하고 있다

---

practice

~~Instead~~, copper and nickel ~~over like~~ gold will be ~~showed~~ stronger in next year.

[Suggestion] instead, copper → instead of copper over like gold will be showed   · over safe assets like gold will be showing

mojo

Instead of gold or safe assets, copper or nickel will likely be bullish in upcoming next year.

[tip] will likely be bullish 강세를 보일 가능성이 있다

upcoming next year 다가오는 내년

text	방아쇠는 당겨졌다. 총구는 전세계에 흩뿌려진 미국 달러를 향하고 있다. 미국이 의도했는지 아닌지는 중요하지 않다.
try	
	[word] 총구 **muzzle** 흩뿌려진 미국 달러 **scattered across the world**

text	어쨌든 미국은 국제경제의 커다란 흐름을 바꿀 수 있는 힘이 있다.
try	[word] 어쨌든 **whatever is may be** 국제경제 **global economy**

practice

It has been ~~triggered~~. The muzzle of a rife is targeted ~~toward~~ US dollar already spread all over the world. Whether US have

[Suggestion] it has been triggered → it has been pulled is targeted toward → is targeted at

mojo

The trigger has been pulled, pointing to the U.S. dollars scattered across the world. It makes no matter whether the U.S. intends to do it or not.

[tip] the gun has triggered, pointing to the U.S. dollars 방아쇠는 당겨졌고 미국 달러를 향하고 있다

---

practice

Whatever it is, the America has power which ~~makes~~ change big stream of global economy.

[Suggestion] which makes change → which can change

mojo

Whatever it may be, the U.S. has the power to change the big track of global economy.

[tip] has potential power to change the big track 흐름을 바꿀 수 있는 힘이 있다

곱게 나이 드는, 벽돌집이 돌아왔다

인기 시들 20여년 만에 제2전성기
한국 건축물은 조선시대까지 대부분 나무로 지었다.
굴뚝, 담장, 성벽 등을 제외하고 사는 집을 짓는 데
벽돌을 쓰기 시작한 것은 1876년 개항 이후부터다.
서구 문물을 받아들이면서 벽돌 건축이 활발해졌다.
1898년에 준공된 명동성당은 국내 최초의 벽돌 교회다.
붉은 벽돌과 회색 벽돌을 조화롭게 쓴 건물로 정평이 나 있다.
따뜻한 느낌의 벽돌이 다시 주목을 받으며
전원주택에서도 대세다.

text	곱게 나이 드는, 벽돌집이 돌아왔다
try	[word] 곱다 **good · fine** 나이들다 **old** 벽돌집 **brick house**
text	인기 시들 20여년 만에 제2 전성기
try	[word] 인기 시들 · 활기 없는 **lackluster**

42

Brick house of fair years is beginning to come back.

The lackluster brick house sees its best day once again after some 20 years.

Korean buildings were mostly built of wood in the Joseon era. With the exception of the chimney, fence and castle, they started to use bricks to build housing ever after an open port in 1876.

The brick architecture has become brisk as things western were generally accepted in the country.

The Myongdong Cathedral built in 1898 is the first brick-built church in Korea. The church is reputed to be a building harmonized with red colored brick and gray brick. The bricks of warm feeling gaining public attention are now noticeable.

practice	~~What the older is~~ the more charming brick house came back. **[Suggestion] what the older is → getting older and**
mojo	Brick house of fair years is beginning to come back. **[tip] brick house of fair years** 오래된 매력적인 벽돌집 **is beginning to come back** 돌아오고 있다
practice	Brick building runs second heyday after more than 20 years withering.
mojo	The lackluster brick house sees its best day once again after some 20 years. **[tip] the lackluster brick house sees its best day** 활기 없는 벽돌집이 전성기를 맞다

text	한국 건축물은 조선시대까지 대부분 나무로 지었다.
try	

[word] 한국 건축물 **Korean buildings**

text	굴뚝, 담장, 성벽 등을 제외하고 사는 집을 짓는 데 벽돌을 쓰기 시작한 것은 1876년 개항 이후부터다.
try	

[word] 굴뚝 **chimney**   담장 **fence**   1876년 개항 **an open port in 1876**

text	서구 문물을 받아들이면서 벽돌 건축이 활발해졌다.
try	

[word] 서구 문물 **things western**

practice	Korean structure was built ~~with almost~~ wood until Joseon era. **[Suggestion] was built with almost wood → was built of mostly wood**
mojo	**Korean buildings were mostly built of wood in the Joseon era.** **[tip] were mostly built of wood** 대부분 나무로 지었다

practice	Using brick for house, ~~exclude~~ chimney, fence and rampart, started from 1876 after opening Korean ports. **[Suggestion] exclude chimney → excluding chimney**
mojo	**With the exception of the chimney, fence and castle, they started to use bricks to build housing ever after an open port in 1876.** **[tip] with the exception** 제외하면 **started to use bricks** 벽돌을 사용하기 시작하다

practice	The brick building ~~was built actively~~ since this country was allowed to accept Western culture. **[Suggestion] was built actively → was actively built**
mojo	**The brick architecture has become brisk as things western were generally accepted in the country.** **[tip] has become brick** 활발해졌다

text

1898년에 준공된 명동성당은 국내 최초의 벽돌 교회다. 붉은 벽돌과
회색 벽돌을 조화롭게 쓴 건물로 정평이 나 있다.

try

[word] 1898년에 준공된 **built in 1898** 최초의 벽돌 교회 **first brick-built church**
조화롭게 **harmonized**

text

따뜻한 느낌의 벽돌이 다시 주목을 받으며 전원주택에서도 대세다.

try

[word] 따뜻한 느낌 **warm feeling** 전원주택 **rural housing**

practice

The Myeongdong Cathedral built in 1898 is first brick church in Korea. It ~~has reputation o~~f harmonious building with using both red brick and gray one.

[Suggestion] has reputation of → has a reputation for

mojo

The Myongdong Cathedral built in 1898 is the first brick-built church in Korea. The church is reputed to be a building harmonized with red colored brick and gray brick.

[tip] is reputed building harmonized 조화롭게 쓴 건물로 정평이 나다

---

practice

Material of genial brick is interest in building, leading ~~trend~~ in part of rural housing.

[Suggestion] trend → trends (경향)

mojo

The bricks of warm feeling gaining public attention are now noticeable in rural housing.

[tip] the bricks gaining public attention 벽돌이 주목을 받으며

쓰레기를 되가져 갑니다.
자연을 지킵니다.

"그린포인트"(Green Point) 란 국립공원 내 방치된 쓰레기 수거 및
자기 쓰레기 되가져 가는 경우 포인트를 제공받고,
포인트로 공원시설을 이용하거나 상품으로 교환하는 제도입니다.

text	쓰레기를 되가져 갑니다. 자연을 지킵니다.
try	

[word] 쓰레기 waste · trash 되가져 가다 **bring back home** 자연 **nature**

text	"그린포인트"(Green Point)란 국립공원 내 방치된 쓰레기 수거 및 자기 쓰레기 되가져 가는 경우 포인트를 제공받고, 포인트로 공원시설을 이용하거나 상품으로 교환하는 제도입니다.
try	

[word] 그린포인트 **Green Point** 방치된 쓰레기 **left litters** 공원시설 **park facility**

43

We must not leave trash behind, preserving the nature.

"Green Point" is a new system aimed for the cases when you collect refuse from the national parks or take them with you, you can get the point and use it for park's facilities when you visit there or change it for gifts.

practice	Let us bring our trash back home.
	Keep our nature from damaging.
mojo	We must not leave trash behind, preserving the nature.
	[tip] **leave trash behind** 뒤에 남겨 두다 **preserve nature** 자연을 보호하다

practice	The Green Point is one of system that visitor gets point when he takes away left litters in the National Park or brings it back home, so that the point can be used in facility of park or changed for gifts.
mojo	"Green Point" is a new system aimed for the cases when you collect refuse from national parks or take them with you, you can get the point and use it for park's facilities when you visit there or change it for gifts.
	[tip] **collect refuse** 쓰레기 수거

불쌍해야만 살아남는 사람들

한 대통령의 삶에 뒤엉킨 혼란과 불행은 강력한 무기였다.
2012년 대선 당시 TV 광고는 60초 중 50초를 커터칼 피습을 당했던
그 후보와 흉터를 보여주는 데 할애했다.
흉터의 길이와 깊이가 표로 이어진단 걸 알았기에 조명도 깊었다.
"너무 불쌍하다"며 많은 이들은 표를 줬다.
이번 게이트의 와중에 또다시 "불쌍함" 카드를 꺼내 들었다.
"가족 간 교류마저 끊고 외롭게 지내왔다." "제가 가장 힘들었던 시절에
곁을 지켜주었다."라고.
삶의 질곡으로 사실을 반박할 순 없다.
시련이 능력을 담보하는 것도 아니다.
하지만 불쌍함을 배배 꼬아 늘려야만 부도덕함과 무능을 덮을 수 있다는 걸
정치인, 재벌 총수나 흉악범들은 알고 있다.
불쌍함을 광고하는 이들은 실제로 불쌍하지 않은 사람들이다.

text	불쌍해야만살아남는 사람들
try	[word] 불쌍하다 **poor · pity** 살아남는 사람 **survive people**
text	한 대통령의 삶에 뒤엉킨 혼란과 불행은 강력한 무기였다.
try	[word] 대통령의 삶 **president life** 뒤엉킨 **mix** 혼란과 불행 **confusion and unhappy** 강력한 무기 **strong arms**

44

Mojo Writing

The people could survive only when they are poor.

President's life entangled with some confusion and misery was her strong weapons to live through them. In 2012 leading up to the presidential campaign, a TV ad spent 50 of 60 seconds to show the candidate attacked with cutter knife, and the scar cut on her face to the audience. When the audience got to realize how the length of the cut scar and its depth would boil down to the ballot, the scar was visibly spotlighted. Many of them cast their votes for her out of pity. Amid the scandal in question, they have drawn the pity card for her again. "I lived a lonely life, alienating myself from my kin and she was always with me when I was alone" said the president.

We can't start refute the way she lived through life's ordeal. The ordeal can't guarantee her ability. Yet politicians, plutocrats and vicious criminal rings know that they can cover up their immorality and do nothing only if they twist the pity on themselves into them being enlarged. Advertising "pity" they are not actually poor as much.

practice	People survived ~~are~~ only if they are looked poor. **[Suggestion] they are looked poor → they looked poor**
mojo	**The people could survive only when they are poor.** **[tip] only when** 이럴 때만
practice	Mixed confusion and ~~unhappy~~ in a president life made a strong arms. **[Suggestion] confusion and unhappy → confusion and unhappiness**
mojo	**President's life entangled with some confusion and misery was her strong weapons to live through them.** **[tip] entangled** 뒤엉킨 **misery** 불행·비참·고통 **weapon** 무기 **to live through them** 무기 삼아 살아갈

text	2012년 대선 당시 TV 광고는 60초 중 50초를 커터칼 피습을 당했던 그 후보와 흉터를 보여주는 데 할애했다.
try	

[word] 대선 **presidential campaign** TV광고 **TV commercial** 커터칼 **cutter knife** 피습을 당하다 **be attacked** 후보 **candidate** 흉터 **scar** 할애하다 **allot**

text	흉터의 길이와 깊이가 표로 이어진단 걸 알았기에 조명도 깊었다. "너무 불쌍하다"며 많은 이들은 표를 줬다.
try	

[word] 길이와 깊이 **length and depth** 표 **ballot** 이어지다 **bring to** 조명 **spotlight** 길다 **long** 표를 주다 **cast vote**

text	이번 게이트의 와중에 또다시 "불쌍함" 카드를 꺼내 들었다. "가족 간 교류마저 끊고 외롭게 지내왔다." "제가 가장 힘들었던 시절에 곁을 지켜주었다."라고.
try	

[word] 게이트 **scandal** 와중에 **amid** 꺼내 들다 **pull out and hold up** 불쌍함 **pathetic** 끊다 **quit** 가족 간 교류 **interaction with family** 외롭게 **lonely** 힘들었던 시절 **in hardest plight**

practice

At the Presidential campaign in 2012, the candidate's scene ~~in which~~ being attacked with a cutter knife, was allotted 50 of 60 seconds on a TV commercial.

[Suggestion] scene in which → scene,

mojo

In 2012 leading up to the presidential campaign, a TV ad spent 50 of 60 seconds to show the candidate attacked with cutter knife, and the scar cut on her face to the audience..

[tip] leading up 이끌던 **ad** 광고 **spend** 보내다 **candidate (who was) attacked scar cut** 잘린 흉터 **audience** 시청자

---

practice

Because the campaign aides knew the scar's length and depth would bring ~~to~~ ballot, they spotlighted it longer. Many should cast vote for the runner, saying "how pity the situation is."

[Suggestion] would bring to ballot → would bring ballot

mojo

When the audience got to realize how the length of the cut scar and its depth would boil down to the ballot, the scar was visibly spotlighted. Many of them cast their votes for her out of pity.

[tip] got to realize 알게 되다 **boil down** 결과가 되다 **visible** 눈에 띄게

vote for her out of pity 불쌍함에 표를 주다

---

practice

Amid ~~in~~ this scandal, the president pulls out and holds up the card of "pathetic" once again, saying "I am living lonely even quitting interaction with my family," "~~during~~ I was in hardest plight, the person took care of me around.

[Suggestion] amid in this scandal → amid this scandal

during I was → when I was

mojo

Amid the scandal in question, they have drawn the pity card for her again. "I lived a lonely life, alienating myself from my kin and she was always with me when I was alone" said the president.

[tip] scandal in question 게이트 와중에 **have drawn** 꺼냈다

alienate 멀리하다 **kin** 친척 · 일가

text

삶의 질곡으로 사실을 반박할 순 없다. 시련이 능력을 담보하는 것도 아니다.

try

[word] 질곡(桎梏: 형구와 수갑, 삶에 대한 속박) **fetter** 반박 **rebut** 시련 **ordeal**
능력 **one's capability** 담보 · 보증 **assure**

text

하지만 불쌍함을 배배 꼬아 늘려야만 부도덕함과 무능을 덮을 수 있다는 걸 정
치인, 재벌 총수나 흉악범들은 알고 있다.

try

[word] 꼬다 **spin** 늘리다 **increase** 부도덕 **immoral** 무능 **inability** 정치인
politician 재벌 총수 **CEO of conglomerate** 흉악범 **vicious criminal**

text

불쌍함을 광고하는 이들은 실제로 불쌍하지 않은 사람들이다.

try

[word] 광고하다 **advertise**

practice With a fettered life, it ~~never would~~ rebut on fact. Ordeal ~~also never is assured~~ one's capability.

[Suggestion] **it never would rebut → it cannot rebut also never is assured → can't assure**

mojo We can't start refute the way she lived through life's ordeal. The ordeal can't guarantee her ability.

[tip] **refute** 반박하다 **guarantee** 보장하다 · 약속하다 · 장담하다

practice However, a few people such as politicians, ~~CEO~~ of conglomerates and vicious criminals, know it good enough that only increasing of hardly spin pity feeling can cover their immoral and inability.

[Suggestion] **CEO → chief · executive officer** 최고 경영자

mojo Yet politicians, plutocrats and vicious criminal rings know that they can cover up their immorality and do nothing only if they twist the pity on themselves into them being enlarged.

[tip] **plutocrat** 부자 · 재벌 · 금권 정치가 **immorality** 부도덕 · 품행이 나쁨 · 악덕 **enlarge** 늘리다 · 확대하다

practice A person who advertises "pity" never be real poor.

mojo Advertising "pity" they are not actually poor as much.

[tip] **actually** 실제로 **as much** 그만큼

병든 화초 '치료'하는 병원 아시나요

서울 관악구에 사는 직장인 김모(40) 씨는 날이 추워지면서
아파트 베란다에서 키우던 바질나무를 이달 초 집안으로 옮겼다.
며칠 지나자 녹색 잎들이 검게 변하며 시들기 시작했다.
김씨는 인터넷상에서 조언을 구하던 중
경기도 농업기술원의 '사이버식물병원'을 알게 됐다.
사진과 함께 진단을 의뢰했다.
하루도 지나지 않아 "흙이 너무 말랐다.
식물이 외부에서 실내로 옮겨지면 호흡이 많아져
수분 부족현상이 더 일어난다.
너무 따뜻한 곳에 둬서는 안되고
겨울철에도 일주일에 한 번 이상 화분 속 흙이 젖을 정도로
물을 줘야 한다"는 연구사의 처방이 왔다.

text	병든 화초 '치료'하는 병원 아시나요
try	
	[word] 병들다 **ailing** 화초 **plant** 병원 **clinic**

text	서울 관악구에 사는 직장인 김모(40) 씨는 날이 추워지면서 아파트 베란다에서 키우던 바질나무를 이달 초 집안으로 옮겼다.
try	
	[word] 직장인 **employee** 날씨 **weather** 추워지다 **getting cold** 베란다 **veranda** 바질나무 **basil tree** 집안 **inside** 이달 초 **early this month**

45

Do you know a clinic which cures ailing plants?

An office worker named Mr. Kim living in Gwanak District, moved a Basil tree from the porch, to the inside of the apartment, as weather began to get cold. A few days later, the green leaves began to turn to black, and wither.

While the Mr. Kim was seeking its caring advice online, he came to hear of 'the cyber plant clinic" of Agricultural Institute in Gyonggi Province. Then with the plant photos, he requested the clinic to checkup the plants. Within a day from it, a research worker sent him a prescription advising that the soil is too dry, the plant requires more moisture to breathe in once the plant is moved from outdoor to indoor, so that the plant may not be placed in to hot place and it must be watered more than once a week so much as the soil in vessel gets wet.

practice	Do you know ~~a kind of~~ hospital treating ailed plant? **[Suggestion] do you know a kind of hospital → do you know hospital**
mojo	**Do you know a clinic which cures ailing plants?** **[tip] cures ailing plants** 병든 화초 치료
practice	Mr. Kim, an employee who is living in Gwanak District, 40, moved a Greek Basil tree into inside from its placed apartment veranda as weather was getting cold early this month.
mojo	**An office worker named Mr. Kim living in Gwanak District, moved a Basil tree from the porch, to the inside of the apartment, as weather began to get cold early this month.** **[tip]** 베란다 **porch**

text

며칠 지나자 녹색 잎들이 검게 변하며 시들기 시작했다.

try

[word] 녹색 잎 **green leave** 검게 변하다 **turn to black** 시들다 **wither**

---

text

김씨는 인터넷상에서 조언을 구하던 중 경기도 농업기술원의 '사이버식물병원'을 알게 됐다.

try

[word] 인터넷상 **online** 조언 **advice** 구하던 중 **while seeking**
농업기술원 **the Institute of Agricultural Techniques**

---

text

사진과 함께 진단을 의뢰했다.

try

[word] 사진 **photo** 진단 **diagnosis** 의뢰

practice

~~Passing~~ several days, the tree's green leaves was turning to black and starting to wither.

[Suggestion] passing several days → after several days

mojo

A few days later, the green leaves began to turn to black, and wither.

[tip] a few days later 며칠이 지나 **began to turn to black** 검게 변하기 시작했다

---

practice

While Mr. Kim was seeking some ~~advices~~ on-line, he knew "cyber plant clinic" the Institute of Agricultural Techniques in Gyonggi Province.

[Suggestion] some advices → some advice

mojo

While the Mr. Kim was seeking its caring advice online, he came to hear of 'the cyber plant clinic" of Agricultural Institute in Gyonggi Province.

[tip] was seeking its caring advices online 인터넷상에서 조언을 구하던 **come to hear** 알게 되다 · 듣게 되다

---

practice

And then he ~~asked diagnosis~~ with its photo at there.

[Suggestion] asked diagnosis → asked for diagnosis

mojo

Then with the plant photos, he requested the clinic to checkup the plants.

[tip] checkup 진단

하루도 지나지 않아 "흙이 너무 말랐다. 식물이 외부에서 실내로 옮겨지면 호흡이 많아져 수분 부족현상이 더 일어난다. 너무 따뜻한 곳에 둬서는 안되고 겨울철에도 일주일에 한 번 이상 화분 속 흙이 젖을 정도로 물을 줘야 한다"는 연구사의 처방이 왔다.

[word] 지나지 않아 **less than a day** 흙 **soil** 호흡 **breathing** 수분부족 **moisture shortage** 일주일에 한번 이상 **more than once a week** 젖다 **wet** 처방 **therapy**

practice

Less than a day, ~~the therapy~~ came from a researcher, saying "soil was too dry to wither. With moving from outdoor to inside, plant increased its breathing and became state of moisture shortage. Avoid it warm place, and pour water until soil in vessel be wet more than once a week during winter season."

[Suggestion] the therapy → the recipe for therapy

mojo

Within a day from it, a research worker sent him a prescription advising that the soil is too dry, the plant requires more moisture to breathe in once the plant is moved from outdoor to indoor, so that the plant may not be placed in to hot place and it must be watered more than once a week so much as the soil in vessel gets wet.

[tip] **within** 이내에 **prescription** 처방 · 지시 **so that something may not be** 하지 않도록 **so much as** 할만큼

서울 밤 풍경은 '비빔밥 빛' 이젠 조명도 우아하게

정미 한국조명디자이너협회장

숭례문, 남산N타워 등 조명 작업

"빛 절제해 쓸 때 정서적 안정감"

조명 디자이너는 '연빛술사'로 빛으로 공간을 창조한다.

조명 디자인의 분야는 조명 기구 디자인과 무대 조명 디자인,

이벤트 조명 디자인 등 다양하지만 최근 새롭게 주목받는 테마는 '사회적 조명'이다.

빛으로 도시의 안전을 확보하며,

도시의 아이덴티티(identity)를 드러내는 작업을 말한다.

text	서울 밤 풍경은 '비빔밥 빛' 이젠 조명도 우아하게
try	
	[word] 밤 풍경 **night scenery** 비빔밥 빛 **admixed coloring lights** 조명 **lighting** 우아하다 **elegant**
text	정미 한국조명디자이너협회장 숭례문, 남산N타워 등 조명 작업 "빛 절제해 쓸 때 정서적 안정감"
try	
	[word] 절제 **refrain · control** 정서적 안정감 **emotional stability**

46

Mojo Writing

Seoul is famous for its night scenes of variety of colors, and for its glaring light.

Jungmi, chief of Illumination designer association with moderate light in lighting working for the Sungyemun and Namsan Tower N, their emotional composure is secured.
A light designer asan alchemist creates a space with the light of. The field of the light design includes various parts of illumination equipment, state lighting design and event lighting design, but the new theme in recent spotlight is "Societal Lighting."Which represents identity of a city by securing stability of the city.

practice	Seoul night scenery is "admixed coloring lights," and now it is ~~going elegantly~~. **[Suggestion] is going elegantly → is becoming elegant**
mojo	**Seoul is famous for its night scenes of variety of colors, and for its glaring light.** **[tip] is famous for** 이름이 나다 · 유명하다 **variety of colors** 다양한 색상 **glaring** 눈부신 · 화려한
practice	Jung Mi who is the Chief of Illumination designer association and worked lighting of Sungnyemun and Namsan N Tower, said "when light is controlled to use, it shows emotional stability."
mojo	**Jungmi, chief of Illumination designer association" with moderate light in lighting working for the Sungyemun and Namsan Tower N, their emotional composure is secured.** **[tip] moderate light** 온화한 빛 **emotional composure** 정서적 침착

text

조명 디자이너는 '연빛술사'로 빛으로 공간을 창조한다.

try

[**word**] 조명 디자이너 **lighting designer** 연금술사 **alchemist** 공간 **space**

text

조명 디자인의 분야는 조명 기구 디자인과 무대 조명 디자인, 이벤트
조명 디자인 등 다양하지만 최근 새롭게 주목받는 테마는 '사회적 조명'이다.

try

[**word**] 분야 **field** 조명 기구 **illuminator** 다양하다 **diverse** 주목 **spolight**

text

빛으로 도시의 안전을 확보하며, 도시의 아이덴티티(identity)를 드러내는
작업을 말한다.

try

[**word**] 안전을 확보 **secure stable** 드러내다 **reveal**

practice

Lighting designer is called an alchemist as lighting and makes up for space through light.

mojo

A light designer as an alchemist creates a space with the light of.

[tip] **the light of an alchemist** 빛의 연금술사

---

practice

The field of lighting design is diverse such as illuminator, stage lighting and event lighting, but newly spotlighted theme is societal lighting.

mojo

The field of the light design includes various parts of illumination equipment, state lighting design and event lighting design, but the new theme in recent spotlight is "Societal Lighting."

[tip] **Societal Lighting** 사회적 조명

---

practice

It is able to work that light secures ~~stable city~~ through light and reveals city's identity.

[Suggestion] **stable city → city's stability**

mojo

Which represents identity of a city by securing stability of the city.

[tip] **represent** 나타내다 · 보여주다

복식 호흡 맞추는 오씨네 부자 마음도 부자 됐어요

전 탁구 국가대표 오상은과 아들
종합선수권 첫 부자 복식조 도전
"함께 땀 흘리며 대화 많이 늘어 아들과 관계 좋아져 또다른 수확"
"아빠가 못 이룬 올림픽 금메달 꿈 중국선수 꺾고 제가 이룰거에요"
14일 경기 안양시 호계체육관 탁구장.
30여명의 탁수선수들 사이에서 한 초등학생이 훈련을 하고 있다.
오상은과 준성(10)군은 부자지간이다.
언뜻 보면 지도자와 선수 같았지만
두 사람 모두 정식 등록선수로서
대회 출전을 앞두고 있다.

text	복식 호흡 맞추는 오씨네 부자 마음도 부자 됐어요
try	

[word] 복식 호흡 abdominal breathing 마음 one's heart

47

Mojo Writing

Mr. Ohs, father and son, keeping in step with each other, got their minds rich.

As member of former national table tennis team, Mr. Oh, and his son first challenged the championship competition of overall men's doubles as father and son.

The father says "I had much talk with him with sweat so I became close with him." The son says "I will defeat the Chinese player, and realize my father's dream, winning the Olympic gold medal which my father failed to take."

In the table tennis room, Hogye Gymnasium on this on this month 14th, an elementary schoolchild was seen training among other 30 tennis players. They were the Oh Sangun and his son, 10, Junsung, themselves. At a glance, they looked a trainer and a player, but the two are both registered players about to participate in a competition.

practice	Mr. Ohs, father and son, ~~fitting on~~ abdominal breathing are affluent full in mind. [Suggestion] fitting on → keeping step with
mojo	**Mr. Ohs, father and son, keeping abdominal breathing in step with each other, got their minds rich.** [tip] ckeeping in step with each other 서로의 보조를 맞추며

text

전 탁구 국가대표 오상은과 아들
종합선수권 첫 부자 복식조 도전

try

[word] 탁구 **table tennis** 국가대표선수 **national athlete** 종합선수권 **the all-round championship athlete** 복식조 **men's doubles**

text

"함께 땀 흘리며 대화 많이 늘어 아들과 관계 좋아져 또다른 수확"

try

[word] 함께 **together** 땀 흘리다 **sweat** 대화 **talking** 수확 **gain**

text

"아빠가 못 이룬 올림픽 금메달 꿈 중국선수 꺾고 제가 이룰거에요"

try

[word] 올림픽 금메달 **Olympic gold medal**

<table>
<tr><td>practice</td><td>Former table tennis national athlete, Mr. Oh and <s>his son are</s> challenging at the all-round championships in <s>first</s> father and son pair.
[Suggestion] his son are → his son first are</td></tr>
<tr><td>mojo</td><td>As member of former national table tennis team, Mr. Oh, and his son first challenged the championship competition of overall men's doubles as father and son.
[tip] first challenged the championship competition overall 첫 종합 선수권에 도전</td></tr>
</table>

<table>
<tr><td>practice</td><td>Mr. Oh said "sweating together, we both increased talking each other, and getting premium by better relationships."</td></tr>
<tr><td>mojo</td><td>The father says "I had much talk with him with sweat so I became close with him."
[tip] so I became close with him 그래서 아들과 관계가 가까워졌다</td></tr>
</table>

<table>
<tr><td>practice</td><td>His son said "I will make a <s>dream that</s> my father failed to get Olympic gold medal, defeating Chinese athletes."
[Suggestion] dream that → dream come true that</td></tr>
<tr><td>mojo</td><td>The son says "I will defeat the Chinese player, and realize my father's dream, winning the Olympic gold medal which my father failed to take."
[tip] my father failed to take dream 아빠가 못 이룬 꿈</td></tr>
</table>

<table>
<tr><td>text</td><td>14일 경기 안양시 호계체육관 탁구장.
30여명의 탁수선수들 사이에서 한 초등학생이 훈련을 하고 있다.</td></tr>
<tr><td>try</td><td></td></tr>
</table>

[word] 탁구선수들 사이에서 **in the table tennis players**
한 초등학생 **an elementary schoolchild**

<table>
<tr><td>text</td><td>오상은과 준성(10)군은 부자지간이다. 언뜻 보면 지도자와 선수 같았지만
두 사람 모두 정식 등록선수로서 대회 출전을 앞두고 있다.</td></tr>
<tr><td>try</td><td></td></tr>
</table>

[word] 언뜻 보면 **at a glance**   정식 등록선수 **registered player**
대회 출전 **participate in a competition**

In the table tennis room of the Hogye gymnasium on this month 14th, among 30 table tennis athletes, ~~one~~ elementally student was training. .

[Suggestion] one → a

[tip] **was seen training** 훈련하는 것이 보인다

---

practice

Oh Sangen and Junsung are father and his son. At a glance, they looked like a coach and a player, but the two are both registered players, and are about to participate a game.

They were the Oh Sangun and his son, 10, Junsung, themselves. At a glance, they looked a trainer and a player, but the two are both registered players about to participate in a competition.

[tip] **they looked a trainer and a player** 그들은 지도자와 선수로 보였다

하루 호두 한 줌, 치매 · 심장병 · 대장암 예방 효과

호두를 먹으면 머리가 좋아진다는 말이 있다.
딱딱한 껍질 속 열매 모양이 인간의 뇌를 닮아서 생긴 이야기다.
이유는 다르지만 호두가 머리에 좋다는 말은 사실이다.
다양한 연구를 통해 호두는 인지 기능을 개선하고 치매를 예방한다고 밝혀졌다.
미국 캘리포니아주립대에서 지난해 발표한 연구에 따르면
호두에 포함된 오메가 3 지방산은 알츠하이머 치매의 원인 물질인
'베타아밀로이드'가 뇌에 쌓이는 걸 막는다.

text	하루 호두 한 줌, 치매 · 심장병 · 대장암 예방 효과
try	[word] 호두 **walnut**　치매 **dementia**　심장병 **heart disease**　대장암 **colon cancer**　예방 **prevention**
text	호두를 먹으면 머리가 좋아진다는 말이 있다.
try	[word] 머리 **brain**　머리가 좋아진다 **bright**

Mojo Writing

A handful of walnuts in a day are helpful for the prevention of dementia, heart disease and colon cancer.

It goes saying that eating walnuts helps brain bright. It stems from the story that the nut inside hard shell looks just like the brain of human being. For a different reason, it is true that the walnut is good for brain to work. Many studies found that the walnut improves cognitive function and prevents dementia. According to finding of research by U.S. California State University, the Omega 3 fatty acid included in the walnut inhibits the beta-amyloid causing dementia from piling up inside the brain.

practice	A handful of walnuts in a day help ~~to effect of~~ prevent~~ing~~ from dementia, heart disease and colon cancer. **[Suggestion] help to effect of preventing from → help prevent from**
mojo	**A handful of walnuts in a day are helpful for the prevention of dementia, heart disease and colon cancer.** **[tip] a handful of walnuts** 호두 한 줌 **helpful for the prevention of dementia** 치매 예방에 도움되다
practice	It goes saying that eating walnuts helps brighten of brain.
mojo	**It goes saying that eating walnuts helps brain bright.** **[tip] It goes saying** 말이 있다 · 말이 전해진다

text	"딱딱한 껍질 속 열매 모양이 인간의 뇌를 닮아서 생긴 이야기다.
try	[word] 딱딱한 껍질 **hard shell** 나오다 **come from**
text	이유는 다르지만 호두가 머리에 좋다는 말은 사실이다.
try	[word] 다르다 **differ** 사실 **true**
text	다양한 연구를 통해 호두는 인지 기능을 개선하고 치매를 예방한다고 밝혀졌다.
try	[word] 다양한 연구 **many studies** 인지 기능 **cognitive ability** 개선 **improve**

practice

It comes from shape of ~~net~~ in its harden shell looked near brain.

[Suggestion] net→ nut

mojo

It stems from the story that the nut inside hard shell looks just like the brain of human being.

[tip] stem from 기인하다 · 어디에서 나오다 **look just like** 닮아서

human being 인간

---

practice

The reason is a little differs, but it is true walnut helps brain works.

[Suggestion] the reason is a little differs → the reason is a little different (is differs a little)

mojo

For a different reason, it is true that the walnut is good for brain to work.

[tip] for a different reason 다른 이유로

---

practice

Many studies ~~reported~~ walnut improves cognitive ability and prevents from dementia.

[Suggestion] studies reported walnut → studies reported that walnut

mojo

Many studies found that the walnut improves cognitive function and prevents dementia.

[tip] found 밝혀졌다 **cognitive function** 인지 기능

미국 캘리포니아주립대에서 지난해 발표한 연구에 따르면 호두에 포함된
오메가 3 지방산은 알츠하이머 치매의 원인 물질인 '베타아밀로이드'가
뇌에 쌓이는 걸 막는다.

[word] 연구에 따르면 **according to study** 치매의 원인 물질 **cause dementia**
베타아밀로이드 **beta-amyloid**

According ~~to reported study~~ last year by U.S. California State University, omega 3 fatty acid included walnut prevents beta-amyloid caused dementia to stack in brain.

[Suggestion] to reported study → to study reported

According to finding of research by U.S. California State University, the Omega 3 fatty acid included in the walnut inhibits the beta-amyloid causing dementia from piling up inside the brain.

[tip] included in the walnut 호두에 포함된 inhibit 억제하다

미 해군 '은밀한 침투자' 줌월트(Zumwalt), 태평양 누비는 까닭

레이더에 안 잡히는 스텔스 구축함
돌고래 만큼 조용, 소나도 탐지 불가
기존 전함 찾는 것보다 50배 어려워
중국 전략에 맞설 '게임 체인저'
155mm 함포, 154km까지 정밀타격
4년내 레일건·레이저포 장착 예정
1척당 4조 5000억 원–지난달 배치
해상 전투의 최강자가 나타났다.
지난 10월 15일 취역한 미국 해군의 '줌월트(Zumwalt, DDG-1000)'구축함이다.
줌월트 구축함은 레이더엔 작은 어선 크기로만 보이고
레이저포 등 최신 무기를 장착해
앞으로 해상에서 전투 흐름과 판도를 뒤바꿀
게임 체인저(game changer)가 될 전망이다.
특히 이 구축함은 해군력을 태평양으로 확대하려는
중국의 장기 전략을 가로막는
결정적인 장애물이 될 것으로 보인다.

text	미 해군 '은밀한 침투자' 줌월트, 태평양 누비는 까닭
try	[word] 미해군 은밀한 침투자 **the US covert invader** 줌월트 **Zumwalt**

49

The U.S. 'covert invader' Zumwalt, is wending its way through the Pacific Ocean. Why is it?

It is one of Stealth destroyers, which is never caught on the radar. It keeps as much quiet as a dolphin, so even sonar is impossible to detect it. Now that it is 50 times as much hard as detecting conventional warship, it is a game changer confronting Chinese strategy.

It is scheduled to equip the navy warship gun of 155mm, making possible to hit up to 154km, with a railgun the laser gun, within four years.

The dispatch costs 4.5 trillion won a ship, which was put in position in the last month 15th, being the strongest fighter.

It is U.S. Navy Zumwalt DDG-1000 commissioned in action on the last October 15th. The Zumwalt destroyer appears to be as a small fishing boat on the radar screen. When it is equipped with latest weapon, we expect it to become game changer, shifting the power of war and its scope in the future. The destroyer will act as critical obstacle to Chinese long term strategy to expand its navy power into the Pacific Ocean.

practice	Why the U.S. Navy Zumwalt-class destroyer goes roaming around in Pacific.
mojo	The US'covert invader,' Zumwalt, is wending its way through the Pacific Ocean. Why is it?

[tip] **Zumwalt is wending its way through the Pacific Ocean** 줌월트가 태평양을 누비다

text	레이더에 안 잡히는 스텔스 구축함 돌고래 만큼 조용, 소나도 탐지 불가
try	**[word]** 레이더 radar 스텔스 구축함 **stealth destroyer** 돌고래 **dolphin** 소나·음파탐지기 **sonar**
text	기존 전함 찾는 것보다 50배 어려워
try	**[word]** 기존 전함 **conventional warship**
text	중국 전략에 맞설 '게임 체인저' 155mm 함포, 154km까지 정밀타격 4년내 레일건·레이저포 장착 예정
try	**[word]** 중국 전략 **Chinese strategy** 게임 체인저 **game changer** 함포 **warship gun** 레일건 **railgun** 레이저포 **laser gun**

practice It is a stealth destroyer ~~passing~~ radar, quiet like a dolphin and impossible to detect even sonar.

[Suggestion] passing → not being noticed by

mojo It is one of Stealth destroyers, which is never caught on the radar.

It keeps as much quiet as a dolphin, so even sonar is impossible to detect it.

[tip] as much quiet as a dolphin 돌고래만큼 조용 **it impossible to detect it** 탐지 불가

---

practice It is 50 times harder to find than an existing warship.

mojo Now that it is 50 times as much hard as detecting conventional warship,

[tip] now that 이기 때문에 **as much hard** 만큼 어렵다

conventional 전통적인 · 틀에 박힌 · 진부한

---

practice It is also 'a game changer' equipped 155mm warship guns and 154km accurate blowing against Chinese strategy, moreover, will install rail gun and laser gun within 4years.

mojo It is a game changer confronting Chinese strategy.

It is scheduled to equip the navy warship gun of 155mm, making possible to hit up to 154km, with a railgun the laser gun, within four years.

[tip] confronting strategy 전략에 맞설 **isscheduled to** 예정된

making possible to hit up 정밀타격 가능성을 이루며

<table>
<tr><td>

text

try

</td><td>

1척당 4조 5000억 원–지난달 배치

[word] 지난달 배치 **dispatched in the last month**

</td></tr>
<tr><td>

text

try

</td><td>

해상 전투의 최강자가 나타났다. 지난 10월 15일 취역한 미국 해군의 '줌월트(Zumwalt, DDG–1000)'구축함이다.

[word] 해상 전투 **naval battle** 최강자 **the most stronger**

</td></tr>
<tr><td>

text

try

</td><td>

줌월트 구축함은 레이더엔 작은 어선 크기로만 보이고 레이저포 등 최신 무기를 장착해 앞으로 해상에서 전투 흐름과 판도를 뒤바꿀 게임 체인저(game changer)가 될 전망이다.

[word] 구축함 **warship** 어선 **a small fishing boat** 레이더 **radar screen** 최신 무기 **latest weapon**

</td></tr>
</table>

practice One dispatched in last month is estimated 4.5trillion won per a ship.

mojo The dispatch costs 4.5 trillion won a ship, which was put in position in the last month 15th, being the strongest fighter.

[tip] **the dispatch costs** 배치는 비용이 들다 **which was put in position** 배치되었다

---

practice The most stronger in naval battle ~~has revealed~~, which is the US Navy Zumwalt, DDG-1000, be placed in commission on past October 15th.

[Suggestion] **has revealed → has made its appearance revealed**

mojo It is US Navy Zumwalt DDG-1000 commissioned in action on the last October 15th.

[tip] **commissioned in action** 취역한 · 임무에 종사한

---

practice So Zumwalt warship is seen like a fishing boat by radar and equipped up-end weapons such as laser gun that it will be prospected a game changer switching state and trend of war in maritime.

mojo The Zumwalt destroyer appears to be as a small fishing boat on the radar screen. When it is equipped with latest weapon, we expect it to become game changer, shifting the power of war and its scope in the future.

[tip] **shifting the power of war and its scope** 전투 흐름과 판도를 바꿀

특히 이 구축함은 해군력을 태평양으로 확대하려는 중국의 장기 전략을
가로막는 결정적인 장애물이 될 것으로 보인다.

[word] 특히 first of all

First of all, it seems to decisive obstacle blocking China's long-term strategy.

The destroyer will act as critical obstacle to Chinese long term strategy to expand its navy power into the Pacific Ocean.

[tip] **will act as critical obstacle** 결정적인 장애물로 활동할 것이다

to expand its navy power 그들 해군력을 확대하려는

미·중 전략적 불신이 한·중관계 근간 흔든다

유럽 내 나토의 꾸준한 확장과
미국 미사일 방어 체계 구축이
러시아 반발과 중국의 불신 초래
미국의 아시아 회귀 정책을 중국은 아시아판
나토 확대로 봐
북핵 제거에 소극적 태도 나타내
중국에 대한 '희망적 사고' 버리고 미·중이 펼치는 체스판 보기 위해
우리 시선을 세계로 향하게 해야
북핵과 사드 이슈는 한·중 양자 차원의 문제가 아니다.
북한 외에 미국과 중국이라는 G2의 전략적 이해관계가 복잡하게 얽혀 있어
이에 대한 제대로 된 이해 없이는 문제 해결의 실마리를 찾을 수 없다.
해법의 실타래를 풀기는커녕 오히려 상대에 대한 오해만 증폭시켜
상황을 더 악화시킬 우려가 크다.

text	미·중 전략적 불신이 한·중 관계 근간 흔든다
try	

[word] 전략적 불신 **strategic distrust** 근간 **keynote**

50

The strategic distrust between the U.S. and China is shaking the keynote of the relations of Korea to China.

The steady expansion of NATO in Europe and building of the U.S. defense missile system have invited both Russian backlash and the mistrust of China.

The China sees the US's return to Asia as the Asian's version of NATO, and takes a negative attitude against the elimination of North Korea nuclear development.

Korea must give up all hope for the China, and avert his eyes to the world to watch the chess game played by the U.S. and China.

The issue of North Korean Nuclear development and THAAD are not matter for the mutual countries. Beside the North Korea, the strategic interest between the U.S. and China has become complicated for the issues so it is hardly possible to find the clue that will unravel the case without an explicit understanding of it. Instead of undoing the skein, it could make the situation worse by growing mutual misunderstanding.

practice	Strategic distrust between the U.S. and China is ~~rocking~~ the root and the trunk of ~~relationship~~ of Korea and China. **[Suggestion] rocking** (흔들의자 등) 흔들다 → **shaking relationship**(인간) 관계를 흔들다 관계 → **relations**
mojo	**The strategic distrust between the U.S. and China is shaking the keynote of the relations of Korea to China.** **[tip] is shaking the keynote** 근간을 흔들다

<table>
<tr><td>text</td><td>

유럽 내 나토의 꾸준한 확장과
미국 미사일 방어 체계 구축이 러시아 반발과 중국의 불신 초래

</td></tr>
<tr><td>try</td><td>

</td></tr>
</table>

[word] 나토 **NATO**　꾸준한 확장 **steady expansion**
미사일 방어체계 **the US defense missile system**　불신 **distrust**

<table>
<tr><td>text</td><td>

미국의 아시아 회귀 정책을 중국은 아시아판 나토 확대로 봐
북핵 제거에 소극적 태도 나타내

</td></tr>
<tr><td>try</td><td>

</td></tr>
</table>

[word] 아시아 회귀 정책 **return to Asia**
북핵 제거 **removal of North Korea missile**

<table>
<tr><td>text</td><td>

중국에 대한 '희망적 사고' 버리고 미·중이 펼치는 체스판 보기 위해
우리 시선을 세계로 향하게 해야

</td></tr>
<tr><td>try</td><td>

</td></tr>
</table>

[word] 중국에 대한 희망적 사고 **all hope for the China**　체스판 **the chess game**

| **practice** | Constant extension NATO in Europe and building of the U.S. missiledefense system ~~resulted~~ inbacklash from Russia and distrust from China.
[Suggestion] result in 이런 결과가 되다 → caused |

mojo The steady expansion of NATO in Europe and building of the U.S. defense missile system have invited both Russian backlash and the mistrust of China.

[tip] have invited both Russian backlash and the mistrust of China 러시아 반발과 중국이 불신을 초래하다

---

practice China sees ~~the returning policy to Asia by U.S.~~ as extension of Asian type NATO, so that it appears negative status for removal of North Korea missile.

[Suggestion] the returning policy to Asia by U.S. → the US returning policy to Asia

mojo The China sees the US's return to Asia as the Asian's version of NATO, and takes a negative attitude against the elimination of North Korea nuclear development.

[tip] the Asian's version of NATOversion 아시아판 나토 형태 negative attitude 소극적 태도 the elimination of North Korea nuclear development 북핵개발 제거

---

practice We need to ~~see~~ toward ~~over the world for~~ watching chess game ~~putting~~ U.S.-China, leaving hopeful mind to China.

[Suggestion] to see toward over the world for → to give up an optimism toward China, chess game putting U.S.-China → chess game by U.S.-China

mojo Korea must give up all hope for the China, and avert his eyes to the world to watch the chess game played by the U.S. and China.

[tip] give up all hope 희망을 단념하다 averthis eyes to the world 시선을 세계로 돌리다

text	북핵과 사드 이슈는 한 · 중 양자 차원의 문제가 아니다.
try	

[word] 양자 차원의 문제 **matter for the mutual countries**

text	북한 외에 미국과 중국이라는 G2의 전략적 이해관계가 복잡하게 얽혀 있어 이에 대한 제대로 된 이해 없이는 문제 해결의 실마리를 찾을 수 없다.
try	

[word] 미국과 중국 **G2 · global two** 전략적 이해관계 **the strategic interest**
문제 해결의 실마리를 찾다 **to find a clu**e

text	해법의 실타래를 풀기는커녕 오히려 상대에 대한 오해만 증폭시켜 상황을 더 악화시킬 우려가 크다.
try	

[word] 실타래 **skein** 오해 **misunderstanding** 증폭 **increase**

practice

The issue of NK missile and THAAD isn't matter of only
bilateral ~~between~~ Korea and China.

[Suggestion] → **bilateral Korea and China** 한·중 양국간

mojo

**The issue of North Korean Nuclear development and
THAAD is not matter for the mutual countries.**

[tip] **THAAD is not matter for the mutual countries** 사드는 양국간 문제
가 아니다

---

practice

~~Out of~~ NK, strategic relation of G2, U.S. and China, is tangled
complexly, and hard to find a clue of the matter until we
understand it properly.

[Suggestion] **out of** → **beside**

mojo

**Besides the North Korea, the strategic interest between the
U.S. and China has become complicated for the issues so it
is hardly possible to find the clue that will unravel the case
without an explicit understanding of it.**

[tip] **besides the North Korea** 북한 이외에 **has become complicated** 복
잡하게 얽혔다 **will unravel the case** 문제를 해결할 **without an explicit
understanding** 제대로 된 이해 없이

---

practice

Rather than resolve its entangled bunch, it is likely almost
amplifying misunderstanding and makes ~~worse~~ this situation.

[Suggestion] → **this situation worse**

mojo

**Instead of undoing the skein, it could make the situation
worse by growing mutual misunderstanding.**

[tip] **Instead of undoing the skein** 해법의 실타래를푸는 대신 **make worse**
악화시키다 · 오해를 증폭시키다

올해 경영 도서 키워드는 인간성·노력·공감

다시 사람이다. 올해 경영 분야에서 사랑받은 책들은
인간만이 가진 끈기와 노력, 공감을 전파하고 있다.
미국 펜실베니아대학의 앤절라 더크워스 교수는
『그릿(Grit)』에서 '타고난 재능'과 '후천적 노력' 중
성공을 결정짓는 것은 후자라고 역설한다.
그릿은 목표를 끝까지 이뤄내고야마는 '투지' 정도로 풀이된다.
사실 역경에 굴하지 않는 노력만큼 인간의 위대함을 드러내는 가치도 없다.
더크워스 교수는 '재능×노력=스킬' '스킬×노력=성취'라며
노력의 위대함을 확신한다.

text	올해 경영 도서 키워드는 인간성·노력·공감
try	[word] 경영 도서 management books 키워드 keyword 인간성 humanity 노력 endeavor 공감 empathy
text	다시 사람이다.
try	[word] 다시 again 사람 human

51

Mojo Writing

The keyword of management books this year is humanity, endeavor and empathy.

Once again, it is man. Our beloved books in the management sector in this year are conveying the patience, effort and empathy that only man can possess. The professor of the U.S. Pennsylvania Angela Duckworth claims in his book 'Grit' that his innate talent and acquired effort are decisive in making success. The 'Grit' is construed as a fighting spirit to attaining his goal. Nothing is more worth than one's tenacity of purpose. Professor Duckworth is convinced that the integral talent and effort makes a skill, and the skill and effort makes an achievement, which make a big contribution to the greatness of human being.

practice	The keywords of management publications in this year are humanity, endeavor and empathy.
mojo	**The keywords of management books this year are humanity, endeavor and empathy.**
	[tip] empathy 공감

practice	Human being stands ahead again.
	[Suggestion] → 사람이 다시 앞에 서 있다 라는 의미
mojo	**Once again, it is man.**
	[tip] man 사람

text

올해 경영 분야에서 사랑받은 책들은 인간만이 가진 끈기와 노력,
공감을 전파하고 있다.

try

[word] 사랑받은 **beloved** 끈기 **patience** 노력 **effort** 공감 **empathy**

---

text

미국 펜실베니아대학의 앤절라 더크워스 교수는 『그릿(Grit)』에서
'타고난 재능'과 '후천적 노력' 중 성공을 결정짓는 것은 후자라고 역설한다.

try

[word] 미국 펜실베니아대학의 앤절라 더크워스 교수 **The professor of the U.S.
Pennsylvania Angela Duckworth** 이를 악무는 기개 · 그릿 **grit**

---

text

그릿은 목표를 끝까지 이뤄내고야마는 '투지' 정도로 풀이된다.
사실 역경에 굴하지 않는 노력만큼 인간의 위대함을 드러내는 가치도 없다.

try

[word] 목표 **goal** 투지 **fighting spirit** 역경 **adversity** 위대함 **great**
가치 **worth**

practice

Beloved books of management sector in this year have transmitted ~~endurance having humanity~~, endeavor and empathy.

[Suggestion] endurance having humanity → endurance, that only man has humanity

mojo

Our beloved books in the management sector in this year are conveying the patience, effort and empathy that only man can possess.

[tip] **beloved books of management sector** 경영분야에서 사랑받은 책들 **are conveying** 전파하고 있다 **only man can possess** 인간만이 가질 수 있는

---

practice

The U.S. Pennsylvania University Angela Duckworth professor ~~insists what~~ makes final success for a man between an innate talent and a posteriori endeavor is the later ~~in her new book, GRIT~~.

[Suggestion] insists in her new book, grit, what~

mojo

The professor of the U.S. Pennsylvania Angela Duckworth claims in her book 'Grit' that her innate talent and acquired effort are decisive in making success.

[tip] **Claims in her book** 책 속에서 말한다·역설하다·주장하다 **innate talent** 타고난 재능 **acquired effort** 몸에 익힌 노력 **decisive** 결정적 **make success** 성공하다

---

practice

GRIT is explained as stubbornness which is not fail to realize ~~for~~ one's goal finally.

[Suggestion] to realize for one's goal → to realize one's goal

mojo

The 'Grit' is construed as a fighting spirit to attaining his goal. Nothing is more worth than one's tenacity of purpose.

[tip] **construe** 해석하다·설명하다 **toattain his goal** 목표를 달성하기 위해 **nothing is more worth** 그 이상 가치 있는 것은 없다 **tenacity** 굴하지 않는 노력·끈기

text

더크워스 교수는 '재능×노력=스킬' '스킬×노력=성취'라며 노력의 위대함을
확신한다.

try

[word] 재능 **talent** 노력 **endeavor** 스킬 **skill** 성취 **achievement**

Nothing ~~there~~ is ~~no the greatest~~ worth of human being as much as endeavor unbowed against hardships. The professor convinces the great of endeavor like as 'talent x endeavor = skill''skill x endeavor = achieve.'
[Suggestion] nothing there is no the greatest → nothing is more greater

Professor Duckworth is convinced that the integral talent and effort makes a skill, and the skill and effort makes an achievement, which make a big contribution to the greatness of human being.

[tip] isconvinced 확신하다 **convince** 확신시키다 **the integraltalent** 완전한 · 전체의 · 필수의 소질 **contribution** 기여 · 공헌 **to the greatness of human being** 인간의 위대함에

색소폰 부는 60대 "성인병 하나도 없어요"

은퇴 후 "반려 악기"가 노인 건강 지킴이로 각광받고 있다.
색소폰·기타·피아노 같은 악기를 폼 나게 연주하다 보면
건강이 저절로 따라온다.
우울·불안·초조 같은 마이너스 감정이 해소되는 건 물론이고
인지능력 집중력이 향상돼 치매를 예방한다.
'평생 다뤄본 악기라곤 노래방에서 흔들었던 탬버린이 전부'라는 사람도
쉽게 도전할 수 있다. 나이도 전혀 문제되지 않는다.
서울 강남구 시니어플라자에서 색소폰 강습을 담당하는 김진 강사는
"70~80세 어르신도 석 달이면 한 곡은 거뜬히 배운다"라고 말한다.

text	색소폰 부는 60대 "성인병 하나도 없어요"
try	
	[word] 색소폰 **saxophone** 60대 **the 60s** 성인병 **geriatric diseases**

text	은퇴 후 "반려 악기"가 노인 건강 지킴이로 각광받고 있다.
try	
	[word] 은퇴 **retire** 반려 악기 **the partner instrument** 각광 **spotlight**

52

Mojo Writing

Blowing saxophone at age of 60s, it eliminates 'geriatric diseases.

The partner instrument after retiring is in spotlight as a keeper of health. Playing the musical instrument like saxophone, guitar or piano in the way of holding himself never miss chance to go with health.It will clear up not only depression, unease or anxiety, but also improve cognitive ability and prevent dementia. Even man, who experienced trembling 'tambourine' in a 'Noraebang' Korean commercial singing room, can go for it in easy way. Age is not a problem. Kim Jin, saxophone instructor at the senior plaza, Kangnamgu, Seoul says that the elder in the age of 70s to 80s learn to play it in three month of its beginning.

practice	Making sound of saxophone, the 60s ~~has "no any~~ disease of his health." **[Suggestion] the 60s has "no any disease → the 60s does not have any disease**
mojo	**Blowing saxophone at age of 60s, it eliminates 'geriatric diseases.'** **[tip] blow (악기를) 불다 eliminate 사라지다 · 없애다 geriatric 노인의 · 노인병의**
practice	After retiring, "the partner instrument" ~~has~~ welcomed ~~for senior as a~~ health keeper. **[Suggestion] has welcomed for senior as a → is welcomed for a senior health keeper**
mojo	**The partner instrument after retiring is in spotlight as a keeper of health.** **[tip] be in spotlight 각광을 받다 · 주목받다 as a keeper of health 건강 지킴이로**

text	색소폰·기타·피아노 같은 악기를 폼 나게 연주하다 보면 건강이 저절로 따라온다.
try	
	[word] 악기 musical instrument
text	우울·불안·초조 같은 마이너스 감정이 해소되는 건 물론이고 인지능력 집중력이 향상돼 치매를 예방한다.
try	
	[word] 우울 depression 불안 unease 초조 anxiety 인지능력 cognitive ability
text	'평생 다뤄본 악기라곤 노래방에서 흔들었던 탬버린이 전부'라는 사람도 쉽게 도전할 수 있다.
try	
	[word] 탬버린 tambourine 도전 challenge
text	나이도 전혀 문제되지 않는다.
try	
	[word] 나이 age 문제 problem·matter

practice

Playing the instrument, such as saxophone, guitar and piano, in fairly ~~good brings~~ to tracing people's health naturally.

[Suggestion] good brings → **good way brings**

mojo

Playing the musical instrument like saxophone, guitar or piano in the way of holding himself never miss chance to go with health.

[tip] **in the way of holding oneself** 폼이 나는 식으로 **never miss chance** 절대 기회를 놓치지 않는다 · 저절로 따라 오게 된다

---

practice

Not only is released from minus feeling like depression, fear and jittery, but also is prevented from dementia by raising concentration.

mojo

It will clear up not only depression, unease or anxiety, but also improve cognitive ability and prevent dementia.

[tip] **clear up** 해소되다 **unease or anxiety** 불안 · 초조 **improve cognitive ability** 인지능력이 개선되다

---

practice

Even a person only experiencing trembled tambourine in the ~~Karaoke, it~~ is able easy to challenge.

[Suggestion] Karaoke, it is → **Karaoke, is**

mojo

Even man, who has just experienced trembling 'tambourine' in a 'Noraebang' Korean commercial singing room, can go for it in easy way.

[tip] **has experienced trembling** 흔들어본 적이 있다

gofor it 힘내다 · 도전하다 **in easy way** 쉽게

---

practice

Their ages doesn't matter at all.

mojo

Age is not a problem.

서울 강남구 시니어플라자에서 색소폰 강습을 담당하는 김진 강사는 "70~80세 어르신도 석 달이면 한 곡은 거뜬히 배운다"라고 말한다.

[word] 시니어플라자 **the senior plaza** 강사 **instructor**

practice

At the senior plaza, Gangnagu District, in Seoul, Kim Jin instructor in charge of saxophone says "the aged from 70s to 80s can learn easily one of music ~~for~~ three months."

[Suggestion] one of music for three months → one of music in three months

mojo

Kim Jin, saxophone instructor at the senior plaza, Kangnamgu, Seoul says that the elder in the age of 70s to 80s learns to play a song in three month of its beginning.

[tip] learns to play a song 한 곳 연주를 배운다

in three month of its beginning 시작한지 석 달이면

색백스윙 팔로스루 길이 같게 끊어치지 말고 밀어야

자기만의 루틴 정해 리듬 지켜야
왼손목 꺾으면 빗나가기 쉬워
골프에서 가장 중요한 것 중 하나는 일관성이다.
특히 퍼팅을 할 때 일관성은 무척 중요하다.
'리듬'의 일관성, '템포'의 일관성은 아무리 강조해도 지나치지 않는다.
퍼팅은 스윙 폭이 크지 않기 때문에 리듬과 템포가 흐트러지면
거리를 맞출 수 없고 방향도 미세하게 틀어질 수 밖에 없다.
짧은 거리에서 퍼팅을 할 때는 일관성이 더욱 중요하다.
일관성을 유지할 수 없으면
짧은 거리의 퍼팅도 놓치는 경우가 종종 생긴다.
이렇게 되면 게임 전체의 흐름을 망칠 수도 있다.

text	백스윙 팔로스루 길이 같게 끊어치지 말고 밀어야
try	[word] 백스위 **backswing** 팔스로우 **follow through**
text	자기만의 루틴 정해 리듬 지켜야
try	[word] 루틴 · 정해진 **routine** 리듬 **rhythm**

53

Mojo Writing

The stroke for the backswing and follow through must be given push with same length and no pause.

Self-serving routine practice rule must be made with constant rhythm.

If left hand wrist makes turn, it is easy to stray off. So what's the most important in the golfing is its consistency. First of all, the consistency when putting is most important the collective consistency of rhythm and tempo is not too much to emphasize. Because the movements of putting are very narrow, its rhythm and tempo should be maintained to keep the distance, and its direction may go a minute wrong way. When you attempt to putt from short distance, the coherence matters even more. Once the consistency is missing, you miss the putt now and then, and it could turn out to be complete failure of the game.

practice	The backswing and the follow through must give a push in same length, hitting unstopped it.
mojo	The stroke for the backswing and follow through must be given push with same length and no pause.

[tip] **the stroke for the backswing** 백스위을 위한 타격은 **nopause** 중단 없이

practice	You keep ride on your rhythm setting own routine rule.
mojo	Self-serving routine practice rule must be made with constant rhythm.

[tip] **self-serving** 직접 하는 · 이기적인 **routine practice rule** 정해진 연습규칙

text	왼손목 꺾으면 빗나가기 쉬워
try	
	[word] 왼손목 **left hand wrist**

text	골프에서 가장 중요한 것 중 하나는 일관성이다.
try	
	[word] 가장 중요한 것 **the most important** 일관성 **consistency**

text	특히 퍼팅을 할 때 일관성은 무척 중요하다. '리듬'의 일관성, '템포'의 일관성은 아무리 강조해도 지나치지 않는다.
try	
	[word] 퍼팅 · 밀어던지기 **putting** 템포 · 속도 **tempo**

text	퍼팅은 스윙 폭이 크지 않기 때문에 리듬과 템포가 흐트러지면 거리를 맞출 수 없고 방향도 미세하게 틀어질 수 밖에 없다.
try	
	[word] 스윙 **swing** 흐트러지다 **scatte**

practice	As a left carpal was turned, it is easy to miss.
mojo	**If left hand wrist makes turn, it is easy to stray off.**
	[tip] make turn 꺾으면 · 돌리면 **tostray off** 빗나가다 · 벗어나다

practice	In the golfing, one of the most important is kept consistency.
mojo	**So what's the most important in the golfing is its consistency.**
	[tip] consistency 언행의 일관성 · 모순되지 않는 · 한결 같은

practice	Above all, when you are doing putting, further so is it.
	The consistency in rhythm and tempo cannot stress enough
	to point it.
mojo	**First of all, the consistency when putting is most important the collective consistency of rhythm and tempo is not too much to emphasize.**
	[tip] first of all 특히 **when (you make) putting** 퍼팅을 할 때 **collective consistency of rhythm and tempo** 리듬과 템포의 합해진 일관성 **not too much to** 아무리

practice	Now that putting is not large ~~in its width~~, losing balance of the rhythm and tempo makes hard to match to distance and allows twisting finely its direction.
	[Suggestion] Now that putting is not large, losing
mojo	**Because the movements of putting are very narrow, its rhythm and tempo should be maintained to keep the distance, and its direction may go a minute wrong way.**
	[tip] narrow 좁다 **to keep the distance** 거리 유지
	minute wrong way 미세하게 틀어지다

짧은 거리에서 퍼팅을 할 때는 일관성이 더욱 중요하다.

[word] 짧은 거리 **short distance**

일관성을 유지할 수 없으면 짧은 거리의 퍼팅도 놓치는 경우가 종종 생긴다.
이렇게 되면 게임 전체의 흐름을 망칠 수도 있다.

[word] 놓치다 **miss** 종종 · 때때로 **now and then**

<table>
<tr><td>practice</td><td>Putting at near distance needs far more consistency.</td></tr>
<tr><td>mojo</td><td>When you attempt to putt from short distance, the coherence matters even more.</td></tr>
</table>

practice | Putting at near distance needs far more consistency.

mojo | **When you attempt to putt from short distance, the coherence matters even more.**

[tip] **coherence** (정신적)일관성 · 일치

the coherence matters even more 정신적 일관성은 더 더욱 중요하다

---

practice If it can't keep consistency, you often meet miss a putting even short range. In this case, it is likely to break a whole game process.

mojo **Once the consistency is missing, you miss the putt now and then, and it could turn out to be complete failure of the game.**

[tip] **once** 일단 **now and then** 때때로 · 가끔 · 이따금 **turn out to be** 되다

✏️

카지노 빗장 푼 일본, 내국인 출입 허용 움직임

일본 카지노 해금법 통과, 격변하는 한중일 삼국지
아베, 마카오·한국서 고객 빼내 내수 진작 노려
"한국 시장서 일본으로 최대 7500억원 빠져 나갈 것"
정부 "도박 중독 등 우려 커 규제 완화 쉽지 않다"
2020년 도쿄 올림픽을 전후로
한중일 카지노 삼국지 시대가 열린다.
일본 아베 정부가 밀어붙여온 카지노 허용 법안이
지난 15일 일본 참의원(상원)을 통과한 결과다.
이에 따라 아시아 카지노 업계,
특히 지리적으로 서로 가까운 동북아 시장의
지각변동이 예상된다.

text	카지노 빗장 푼 일본, 내국인 출입 허용 움직임
try	

[word] 카지노 casino 빗장 bar 내국인 local people 허용 allow

54

Mojo Writing

With lifting barring from casino, Japan is moving to allow its local people to make access to it.

Japan has passed the law to lift the ban, which foresees potentially sudden change of the triple countries, Korea, China and Japan.
Abe seeks to take customers from Macao and Korea to stimulate his domestic consumption.
At most 750 billion won will possibly be leaving Korean market.
Government says that is not easy to deregulate the casino in the fear of gambling addiction.
About the time of the 2020 Tokyo Olympic Games, the casino competition age of the triple countries is dawning. It is the fruit that the law lifting banning of casino, pushed on by Abe, passed through Japanese Upper House on 15th of the last month.
Along the way, Asian casino industries, the northeastern Asia, geographical neighboring countries, is expected to undergo the late change of its market.

practice	With unbarring casino, Japan moves to allow ~~for~~ people to enter it. **[Suggestion] to allow for people → to allow people**
mojo	**With lifting barring from casino, Japan is moving to allow its local people to make access to it.** **[tip] lift** 해제하다 · 들어 올리다 **bar from** 금지하다 **allow to** 허용하다 **local people** 내국인 **make access to** 들어가다 · 이용하다

text	일본 카지노 해금법 통과, 격변하는 한중일 삼국지
try	[word] 해금법 · 금지를 해제하는 법 **the law to lift the ban**
text	아베, 마카오 · 한국서 고객 빼내 내수 진작 노려
try	[word] 마카오 **Macao** 고객 **customer** 빼내다 **pull out** 진작 · 자극 **stimulate**
text	"한국 시장서 일본으로 최대 7500억 원 빠져 나갈 것" 정부 "도박 중독 등 우려 커 규제 완화 쉽지 않다"
try	[word] 한국시장 **Korean Market** 최대 **at most** 도박 중독 **gambling addiction**

practice

As Japan passed ~~a lifting casino law~~, the situation of Korea, China and Japan is faced to shift.

[Suggestion] a lifting casino law 해제되는 카지노 법 → 다른 의미

mojo

Japan has passed the law to lift the ban, which foresees potentially sudden change of the triple countries, Korea, China and Japan.

[tip] **passed the law to left the ban** 금지해제 법을 통과시켰다 **foresee** 예견하다 · 내다보다 **potentially** 어쩌면 · 아마도 **triple countries** 삼(인조)국

---

practice

Abe aims to ~~domestic stimulate~~, pulling out customers from Macao and Korea.

[Suggestion] to domestic stimulate → to stimulate domestic demand

mojo

Abe seeks to take customers from Macao and Korea to stimulate his domestic consumption.

[tip] **seek to** 노리다 **takecustomer** 고객을 빼내서 **domestic economy** 내수

---

practice

"It will be drained at most up to 750 billion won from Korea to Japanese market."Government said "It may be hard to ease the regulation by raising concern about gambling addiction."

mojo

"At most 750 billion won will possibly be leaving Korean market." Government says "that is not easy to deregulate the casino in the fear of gambling addiction."

[tip] **be leaving** 빠져나갈 **is not easy to deregulate the casino** 카지노 규제완화가 쉽지 않다 **in the fear of** 우려 **gambling addiction** 도박 중독

text	2020년 도쿄 올림픽을 전후로 한중일 카지노 삼국지 시대가 열린다.
try	

[word] 도쿄 올림픽 **Tokyo Olympic**　카지노 삼국지 **the triple countries of casino**

---

text	일본 아베 정부가 밀어붙여온 카지노 허용 법안이 지난 15일 일본 참의원(상원)을 통과한 결과다.
try	

[word] 아베 정부 **Abe administration**　밀어붙이다 **push on**　일본 참의원·상원 **Japanese Upper House**

---

text	이에 따라 아시아 카지노 업계, 특히 지리적으로 서로 가까운 동북아 시장의 지각변동이 예상된다.
try	

[word] 이에 따라 **along the way**　아시아 카지노 업계 **the Asian casino industry**
동북아 **the northeastern Asia**　지각변동 **crustal movements**

practice

When ~~it comes to hold~~ Tokyo Olympic in 2020, time will open the competition of casino version among three nations.

[Suggestion] **when it comes to hold tokyo olympic in 2020, → when tokyo olympic is held in 2020,**

mojo

About the time of the 2020 Tokyo Olympic Games, the casino competition age of the triple countries is dawning.

[tip] **The age is dawning** 시대가 시작하다 · 열리다 **dawn** 새벽

---

practice

Having pushed ~~to allow~~ by Japanese Abe administration, the casino law resulted in passing through the Upper House on last month 15th in Japan.

[Suggestion] **having pushed to allow by → having pushed by**

mojo

It is the fruit that the law lifting banning of casino, pushed on by Abe, passed through Japanese Upper House on 15th of the last month.

[tip] **it is the fruit** 결과다 **the law lifting banning of casino** 카지노 금지를 해제하는 법 **pushed on by Ave** 아베가 밀어붙여왔던

---

practice

The Asian casino industry along with it, it is expected to change in its northeastern market in particular nearest geography.

mojo

Along the way, Asian casino industries, the northeastern Asia, geographical neighboring countries, is expected to undergo upheaval of its market.

[tip] **geographical neighboring countries** 지리적으로 가까운 **undergoupheaval** 지각변동을 겪다

미국의 자유로움 펼친듯한 컬렉션장

뉴욕 아이덴티티 담은 웅장한 피날레

코치, 2017 여성 Pre Fall 쇼 & 남성 Fall 쇼 선보여

모던 럭셔리 브랜드 코치에서 올해 75주년의 대미를 장식하기 위해

2017 여성 Pre Fall 쇼와 남성 Fall 쇼를 선보였다.

뉴욕 Pier 94에 위치한 웅장한 스튜디오는

미국 전형의 자유로움을 상징하는 듯 넓은 광야를 표현하는

컬렉션장으로 탈바꿈했다.

이번 쇼는 50명의 남녀 모델들이 함께 레트로 콘셉트의

빈티지한 컬렉션을 복고풍의 음악에 맞춰

더욱 강렬하게 선보였다.

text	미국의 자유로움 펼친듯한 컬렉션장
try	[word] 자유로움 **freedom** 펼치다 **unfold** 컬렉션장 **a collection runway**
text	뉴욕 아이덴티티 담은 웅장한 피날레
try	[word] 뉴욕 아이덴티티 **the identity of New York** 피날레 **finale**

55

Mojo Writing

A collection runway that apparently looks like unfolding the freedom of America.

It is an imposing finale bearing the identity of New York
Coach exhibits 2017 Women Pre Fall Show and the Men Fall Show.
Modern Luxury Brand Coach introduced the selection of the Women
Pre Fall Show and the Men Fall Show to mark its 75th anniversary.
The magnificent studio, located at Pier 94, New York has been
changed into a collection runway representing an extensive prairie
as if it is symbolizing an American typical freedom.
50 mem and girl models who were featured in the show introduced
a mighty vintage collection of retro concept in line with revival
music.

practice	A collection runway seen like ~~unfolded~~ the freedom of America **[Suggestion] like unfolded → like unfolding**
mojo	A collection runway that apparently looks like unfolding the freedom of America. **[tip] that apparently looks like unfolding the freedom** 그것은 분명히 자유를 펼친듯이 보인다
practice	It has been a grand finale ~~brought~~ New York identity. **[Suggestion] finale brought → finale bring**
mojo	It is an imposing finale bearing the identity of New York **[tip] it is an imposing finale** 피날레에 적용하고 있다 **bearing the identity of New York** 뉴욕 아이덴티티를 담은

text	코치, 2017 여성 Pre Fall 쇼 & 남성 Fall 쇼 선보여
try	[word] 코치 **Coach**
text	모던 럭셔리 브랜드 코치에서 올해 75주년의 대미를 장식하기 위해 2017 여성 Pre Fall 쇼와 남성 Fall 쇼를 선보였다.
try	[word] 모던 럭셔리 브랜드 **Modern Luxury Brand**
text	뉴욕 Pier 94에 위치한 웅장한 스튜디오는 미국 전형의 자유로움을 상징하는 듯 넓은 광야를 표현하는 컬렉션장으로 탈바꿈했다.
try	[word] 스튜디오 **studio**　전형 **typical**　넓은 광야 **extensive prairie**

practice

Coach exhibits the Women Pre Fall 2017 show and the Men Fall show.

mojo Coach exhibits 2017 Women Pre Fall Show and the Men Fall Show.

[tip] **exhibit** 선보이다

---

practice

The modern luxury brand of Coach released the Women Pre Fall 2017 show and the Men Fall show in order to decorate of the greatest ending for 75 years in this year.

mojo Modern Luxury Brand Coach introduced the selection of the Women Pre Fall Show and the Men Fall Show to mark its 75th anniversary.

[tip] **to mark its 75th anniversary** 75주년을 기념하기 위해

---

practice

A majestic studio located ~~in~~ Pier 94, New York has turned into a collection runway which imagines broad prairie symbolized freedom of typical the U.S.

[Suggestion] **located in pier 94 → located at pier 94**

mojo The magnificent studio, located at Pier 94, New York has been changed into a collection runway representing an extensive prairie as if it is symbolizing an American typical freedom.

[tip] **magnificent studio** 웅장한 스튜디오 **has been changed into a collection runway** 컬렉션장으로 탈바꿈했다

이번 쇼는 50명의 남녀 모델들이 함께 레트로 콘셉트의 빈티지한 컬렉션을
복고풍의 음악에 맞춰 더욱 강렬하게 선보였다.

[word] 레트로 콘셉트 · 복고풍 개념 **retro concept**

This time showed 50 men and women models expressed mighty collection of retro concept vintage style matching on revival music.

50 mem and girl models who were featured in the show introduced a mighty vintage collection of retro concept in line with revival music.

[tip] **Who were featured in the show** 쇼에 출연한 사람 **introduced a mighty vintage collection** 강한 빈티지 컬렉션을 선보였다

유방암 완치율, 미국보다 높은 92%… 환자 마음까지 어루만지다

이대여성암병원 유방암센터의 완치율(5년 생존율)은 92%로
국내 평균은 물론 미국(89%)보다 높다.
재발률도 3% 이하로 세계 최저 수준이다.
이런 배경에는 나름의 수술 노하우가 있다.
유방은 중심 부위에서 유방 전체로 뻗은 15개의 유선(乳腺) 가지들이 있다.
이곳 어느 한 부위 또는 여러 군데에 암이 생긴다.
그러면 해당 부위뿐 아니라 가지를 따라 암세포가 이동하기 쉽다.
 따라서 유방 암 수술 땐 암이 생긴 가지를 따라
암 조직을 잘 걷어내는 것이 관건이다.
너무 많이 걷어 내면 유방 형태를 보존할 수 없고,
너무 적게 걷어내면 암세포가 남아 있을 수 있어
남다른 노하우가 필요하다.

text	유방암 완치율, 미국보다 높은 92%… 환자 마음까지 어루만지다
try	

[word] 유방암 **breast cancer** 완치율 **recovery rate** 환자 **patient**

56

Mojo Writing

The recovery rate of breast cancer is 92%, higher than that of the U.S., soothing patients' mind.

The Center of Breast Cancer of Iwha Women Cancer Hospital boasts an average rate (5 years survival) of 92%, which is higher than that of the U.S, 89%. Its returning rate is under 3%, which is the lowest in the world. Korea has know-how background to support the treatment of breast cancer. Breast has 15 mammary glands stretching around the breast from the center of breast. Cancer can occur at one or more parts of the glands. Then cancer cells can easily move along the affected regions or the branches of the glands, so that it is pivotal point to trace the origin of cancer and remove successfully the cancer tissues. An excessive removal of the affected tissue can deform the breast shape, or the least removal of them may let the cancer tissue stay. It, therefore, requires an unique know-how to deal with it.

practice	The recovery rate of breast cancer is ~~higher to 92% than~~ the U.S. ratio, even soothing patients down. **[Suggestion] is higher to 92% → is 92% higher than**
mojo	The recovery rate of breast cancer is 92%, higher than that of the U.S., soothing patients' mind. **[tip] soothing patient's mind 환자 마음까지 어루만진다**

text	이대여성암병원 유방암센터의 완치율(5년 생존율)은 92%로 국내 평균은 물론 미국(89%)보다 높다.
try	**[word]** 이화여성암병원 **Iwha women cancer hospital** 평균 **average**

text	재발률도 3% 이하로 세계 최저 수준이다.
try	**[word]** 재발률 **recurrence rate** 최저 수준 **lowest level**

text	이런 배경에는 나름의 수술 노하우가 있다.
try	**[word]** 배경 **background**

text	도쿄 올림픽을 전후로 한중일 카지노 삼국지 시대가 열린다. 유방은 중심 부위에서 유방 전체로 뻗은 15개의 유선(乳腺) 가지들이 있다.
try	**[word]** 유방 **breast** 15개의 유선 **mammary glands**

practice

The recovery rate of breast cancer for survival ~~rate through~~ last five years in the center of breast cancer of Iwha women cancer ~~hospital is high not only local average, but also the U.S. one, 89%~~.

[Suggestion] rate through → **rate 92% through**

cancer hospital local average, is higher than the US 89%.

mojo

[tip] **boasts an average rate of 92%** 평균 92%율을 자랑한다

---

practice
mojo

Its recurrence rate is also lowest level at 3% in the world.

Its returning rate is under 3%, which is the lowest in the world.

[tip] **Its returning rate is under 3%** 재발률도 3% 이하다

---

practice

It hangs on an operational know-how ~~in~~ background.

[Suggestion] **know-how in background → know-how background**

mojo

Korea has know-how background to support the treatment of breast cancer.

[tip] **has know-how background to support** 지원할 배경 노하우가 있다

---

practice

Breast has 15 mammary glands spreading from center to overall.

mojo

Breast has 15 mammary glands stretching around the breast from the center of breast.

[tip] **stretching around the breast** 유방 주위로 뻗어있는

text	이곳 어느 한 부위 또는 여러 군데에 암이 생긴다.
try	
	[word] 한 부위 one part

text	그러면 해당 부위뿐 아니라 가지를 따라 암세포가 이동하기 쉽다. 따라서 유방 암 수술 땐 암이 생긴 가지를 따라 암 조직을 잘 걷어내는 것이 관건이다.
try	
	[word] 가지를 따라 **along the branches** 암 수술 **cancer surgery** 암 조직 **cancer tissue**

text	너무 많이 걷어 내면 유방 형태를 보존할 수 없고, 너무 적게 걷어내면 암세포가 남아 있을 수 있어 남다른 노하우가 필요하다.
try	
	[word] 유방 형태 **the breast shape** 보존하다 **keep · preserve**

practice

A cancer usually occurs at one or more of glands.

mojo

Cancer can occur at one or more parts of the glands.

[tip] **occur at one or more parts** 한 부위 또는 여러 군데에 생긴다

practice

So some cancer cells as well as original part are easy to move through the glands. What is a key point when the breast cancer operates is to be removed cancer tissues created along with the glands.

mojo

Then cancer cells can easily move along the affected regions or the branches of the glands, so that it is pivotal point to trace the origin of cancer and remove successfully the cancer tissues.

[tip] **move along the affected regions** 가지를 따라 이동 **it is pivotal point** 주요 관건이다 **to trace the origin of cancer and remove** 암이 생긴 자리를 추적하고 제거하는 것이

practice

If it is dipped up ~~much~~, the shape of breast is hard to form, and if it is scooped up small, the cancer tissue can be left. It means to need peculiar know-how.

[Suggestion] **is dipped up much → is dipped up too much**

mojo

An excessive removal of the affected tissue can deform the breast shape, or the least removal of them may let the cancer tissue stay. It, therefore, requires an unique know-how to deal with it.

[tip] **An excessive removal of the affected tissue** 영향 받은 조직의 과도한 제거 **can deform** 형태가 변형될 수 있다 **requires an unique know-how** 남다른 독특한 노하우가 필요하다

"4년 만에 독자 2000만, 비결은 재미있게 쓰는 것"

미 온라인매체 '쿼츠' 딜레이니 편집장
"모바일시대 맞게 콘텐츠 공급
갭 실적발표 기사, 패션기자가 써
250단어 내외로 독자와 얘기하듯"
2012년 출범한 미국의 쿼츠(Quartz)는
모바일에 최적화된 디지털 실험을 주도하며
급성장한 온라인 경제매체다.
올 초 선보인 아이폰앱은
독자와 문자를 주고 받는 채팅 앱을 지향한다.
"우선 모바일 최적화 콘텐트를 만들고 시간이 남으면 PC용으로 만든다.
4년 전부터 미래 성장동력은 모바일에 있고,
소셜미디어 시대에는 홈페이지도 필요없다고 봤다."

text	"4년 만에 독자 2000만, 비결은 재미있게 쓰는 것" 미 온라인매체 '쿼츠' 딜레이니 편집장
try	

[word] 독자 reader 비결 secret·key 온라인 매체 online media 쿼츠 Quartz

57

Mojo Writing

"Already having 20 millions of reader in four years, a secret of the writer is to write an interesting story" said the U.S. online media 'Quartz' editor in chief, Delaney.

A fashion writer came up with an article about the results of 'Gap' and said, "They write book in a vocabulary of 25 words just like talking with readers."
The U.S. online media 'Quartz' is one of the online economies, which was launched in 2012, and has grown into leading a digital experiment optimized with mobile. The iPhone App, introduced early in this year, is pointing to a kind of chatting App to make it possible to exchange text message with its reader. The 'Quartz concludes, "we work with the aim of making contents of optimization of mobile and if time is left lead time, we would make some for PC. It already foresaw the mobile as growth engine four years before, the homepage would be no more needed in the age of social media.

practice	"The way of making 20 Million Reader in four years is ~~writing~~ for fun."The U.S. online media 'Quartz' editor in chief, Kevin J. Delaney, says **[Suggestion] is writing → is to write**
mojo	**"Already having 20 millions of reader in four years, a secret of the writer is to write an interesting story" said the U.S. online media 'Quartz' editor in chief, Delaney.** **[tip] a secret of the writer** 저자의 비결 **interesting story** 재미있는 이야기

text	"모바일시대 맞게 콘텐츠 공급 갭 실적발표 기사, 패션기자가 써 250단어 내외로 독자와 얘기하듯"
try	
	[word] in line with ~에 따라

text	2012년 출범한 미국의 쿼츠(Quartz)는 모바일에 최적화된 디지털 실험을 주도하며 급성장한 온라인 경제매체다.
try	
	[word] 최적화된 **optimized**　디지털 실험 **digital experiment**

text	올 초 선보인 아이폰앱은 독자와 문자를 주고 받는 채팅 앱을 지향한다.
try	
	[word] 지향하다 **intend**　채팅 앱 **chatting App**

"We offer contents in line with mobile era, for example, report of Gap earning data, social news by fashion reporter, article about 250 words that is like talking with reader."

"A fashion writer came up with an article about the results of 'Gap' and said, "They write book in a vocabulary of 25 words just like talking with readers."

[tip] **come up with an article** 기사를 내놓다 · 해내다 **just like talking with readers** 독자와 이야기하듯

Launching in 2012, Quarts of the U.S. is online economic media emerging and leading on optimized digital experiment at mobile.

The U.S. online media 'Quartz' is one of the online economies, which was launched in 2012, and has grown into leading a digital experiment optimized with mobile.

[tip] **was launched** 출범했다 **has grown into leading** 이끌도록 성장했다

The iphone App introduced ~~early this~~ year intends a kind of chatting App exchanging message by text.

[Suggestion] **early this year → early in this year**

The iPhone App, introduced early in this year, is pointing to a kind of chatting App to make it possible to exchange text message with its reader.

[tip] **is pointing to** 지향하고 있다

it possible to exchange text message 문자 교환이 가능한

<table>
<tr><td>text</td><td>“우선 모바일 최적화 콘텐트를 만들고 시간이 남으면 PC용으로 만든다.</td></tr>
<tr><td>try</td><td>

[word] 최적화 **optimized**</td></tr>
<tr><td>text</td><td>4년 전부터 미래 성장동력은 모바일에 있고, 소셜미디어 시대에는
홈페이지도 필요없다고 봤다.”</td></tr>
<tr><td>try</td><td>

[word] 성장동력 **growth engine**　소셜미디어 시대 **the age of social media**</td></tr>
</table>

"We make first optimized content at mobile, and for PC one is next in the rest time.

The 'Quartz concludes, "we work with the aim of making contents of optimization of mobile and if time is left lead time, we would make some for PC.

[tip] **The aim of making contents** 콘텐츠를 만드는 것이 목표

optimization of mobile 모바일에 최적화

with possible lead time 기다리는 시간이 있다면

We see mobile as growth engine of industry from four years ~~age~~, and no needs even a homepage in the social media era."

[Suggestion] **from four years age** → **from four years ago**

It already foresaw the mobile as growth engine four years before, the homepage would be no more needed in the age of social media.

[tip] **foresee** 내다보다 · 예견하다 **no more needed** 더 이상 필요없다

채식자용 '콩고기 버거'(임파서블 버거), 빌 게이츠·리카싱도 투자

쑥쑥 크는 '베지노믹스'
콩·아몬드·참깨로 육즙까지 재현
구글서 3억 달러에 인수 제의도
"진짜 닭고기와 구분 불가능"
'비욘드 미트'엔 육류회사도 투자
달걀 대신 식물로 만든 마요네즈
유제품 함량 0% 초콜릿도 나와
채식주의자가 늘어나고 있다. 채식을 선택하는 이유는 제각각이다.
빌클린턴(70) 전 미국 대통령은 세 번의 수술을 경험한 뒤 채식주의자가 됐다.

text	채식자용 '콩고기 버거'(임파서블 버거), 빌 게이츠·리카싱도 투자
try	
	[word] 채식자 **vegetarian**·**vegan** 빌 게이츠 **Bill Gates** 리카싱 **Li Kashing**

text	쑥쑥 크는 '베지노믹스' 콩·아몬드·참깨로 육즙까지 재현 구글서 3억 달러에 인수 제의도
try	
	[word] 쑥쑥 크다·빨리자라다 **fast growing** 콩 **bean** 아몬드 **almond** 참깨 **sesame**

58

In the 'soy meat' named impossible burger, for vegetarian, even Bill Gate and one of business magnate Li Ka-shing have invested.

Fast growing 'Veganomics' has reproduced even meat juice with bean, almond and sesame. Google offered to acquire it for $300 million. "It is all but impossible to tell real chicken from it." 'Beyond Meat' is invested by meat companies. Even mayonnaise is made from plants instead egg, and chocolate with no content of dairy is coming up. The number of vegetarian is growing. The reason for choosing vegan diet differs each. The former U.S. president Bill Clinton is now one of vegetarian after undergoing surgeries three times.

practice	'Soy meat, named impossible burger, for vegetarian is invested by Bill Gates and business magnate Li Ka-shing.
mojo	In the 'soy meat,' named impossible burger, for vegetarian, even Bill Gate and one of business magnate Li Ka-shing have invested.

[tip] **soy meat or soya chunks** 콩고기 **invested in** ~에 투자하다 **business magnate** 재계의 거물

practice	Growing 'veganomics' quickly reproduces even broth with bean, almond and sesame, getting ~~to propose~~ of acquisition for $300 million from Google.

[Suggestion] **getting to propose → getting proposal**

mojo	Fast growing 'Veganomics' has reproduced even meat juice with bean, almond and sesame. Google offered to acquire it for $300 million.

[tip] **Veganomics** 채식자의 생활과 건강향상에 관계하는 온라인 매체 **reproduce meat juice with bean** 콩으로 육즙까지 재현하다

text	"진짜 닭고기와 구분 불가능"
try	[word] 진짜 **real** 닭고기 **chicken** 구분 **separation**
text	'비욘드 미트'엔 육류회사도 투자
try	[word] 육류회사 **meat companies** 투자 **invest**
text	달걀 대신 식물로 만든 마요네즈 유제품 함량 0% 초콜릿도 나와
try	[word] 식물 **plant** 마요네즈 **mayonnaise** 유제품 **dairy**
text	채식주의자가 늘어나고 있다. 채식을 선택하는 이유는 제각각이다. 빌클린턴 (70) 전 미국 대통령은 세 번의 수술을 경험한 뒤 채식주의자가 됐다.
try	[word] 늘다 **increase** 제각각 다르다 **differ each** 수술 **surgery**

practice	"It is impossible ~~compare to~~ real chicken."
	[Suggestion] **compare to** 비교하다 **is impossible compare to real chicken → is impossible to tell it from rel chicken**
mojo	**"It is all but impossible to tell real chicken from it."**
	[tip] **all but · very nearly · almost** 거의 **to tell ~ from** 구별하다

practice	'Beyond Meat' is invested by the meat companies.
mojo	**'Beyond Meat' is invested by meat companies.**
	[tip] **Beyond Meat-The future of protein**™ 식물성 식재료로 버거, 닭고기, 푸딩, 미트볼을 만드는 회사

practice	There has been mayonnaise made ~~by~~ plant instead of egg and come up chocolate included no dairy.
	[Suggestion] **by → from**
mojo	**Even mayonnaise is made from plants instead egg, and chocolate with no content of dairy is coming up.**
	[tip] **be made from plant** 식물로 만들어진 **content** 함량
	is coming up 나오고 있는 중이다

practice	Vegetarian ~~is getting increase~~. The reason for choosing vegan diet differs each. The former U.S. president Bill Clinton has become a vegetarian after suffering three time surgeries.
	[Suggestion] **is getting increase → is increase**
	is getting increase. The reason → is increasing the reason
mojo	**The number of vegetarian is growing. The reason for choosing vegan diet differs each. The former U.S. president Bill Clinton is now one of vegetarian after undergoing surgeries three times.**
	[tip] **the number of** 숫자 **under go surgeries** 수술을 하다

채식자용 '콩고기 버거'(임파서블 버거), 빌 게이츠·리카싱도 투자

'1초'는 가능하다.

1분은 60초, 1년 하면 3,153만 6천 초인데,

내년은 '인간의 힘으로' 1초를 더해 3,153만 6천1초가 된다.

이렇게 1초를 더하거나 빼는 걸 윤초라고 한다.

2017년은 벌써 28번째인데 왜 이런 현상이 생기는 것일까?

정유년 새해가 시작되는 1월 1일 아침 9시는 1초 늦게 시작된다.

8시 59분 59초에서 9시 정각이 되는 게 아니라

59분 60초, 즉 1초가 추가된 뒤 9시로 넘어간다.

하루 한 바퀴 도는 지구의 자전이 밀물과 썰물,

지진, 화산 활동 등에 의해

미세하게 느려진 게 누적되면서,

항상 일정한 원자시계와 1초 가까운 오차가 발생해,

바로잡는 것이다.

지난 1972년 이후 27차례에 걸쳐 1초씩 늘렸고

이번이 28번째 윤초다.

text	흘러가는 시간을 인간이 조정할 수 있을까? '1초'는 가능하다.
try	

[word] 가는 시간 **the passing time**　조정 **control**

59

Can man control the passing time?

One second is possible to control.

One minute consists of 60 seconds and a year is 31 million and 536 thousand seconds. The next year is added one second by man to be 31 million and 536 thousand and one seconds. Extension or subtracting one second is called a leap second.

The 2017 is 28th year of the occurrence happening. How come is it coming?

The 9 a.m. of January first day of the new year, called 'the Chicken Year,' will start one second late. 9 a.m. on January 1st starting with the Chicken Year comes one minute late. The 9 a.m. doesn't come after 8:59.59., but the 9 a.m. come following 8:60 after one second added to 8:59.59.

With the earth rotation being minutely behind time and accumulated, caused by a rising tide and ebb, earthquake and volcanic activity, the errors in the range of one second are unavoidable on the basis of atomic clock so the error is corrected in the process. One second has been added 27 times since 1972, and 2017 is 28ththe leap year.

practice	Can people controls the passing time?
	One minute is possible to control.
mojo	**Can man control the passing time?**
	One second is possible to control.
	[tip] man control the passing time 사람이 가는 시간을 조정하다

text	1분은 60초, 1년 하면 3,153만 6천 초인데, 내년은 '인간의 힘으로' 1초를 더해 3,153만 6천 1초가 된다.
try	
	[word] 인간의 힘으로 **by man**　더하다 **add**

text	이렇게 1초를 더하거나 빼는 걸 윤초라고 한다.
try	
	[word] 윤초 **a leap second**　더하거나 빼기 **add or subtract**

text	2017년은 벌써 28번째인데 왜 이런 현상이 생기는 것일까?
try	
	[word] 왜 **how come**　현상 **fact · phenomenon**

practice	~~One minute is sixty second~~, a year is 31 million and 536 thousand second; and when the next year is forced one minute to add by human control, it will be 31 million and 536 thousand and one second.

[Suggestion] One minute is sixty second. →There are 60 seconds in a minute.

mojo One minute consists of 60 seconds and a year is 31 million and 536 thousand seconds. The next year is added one second by man to be 31 million and 536 thousand and one seconds.

[tip] consist of 구성되다

addone second by man to be 이렇게 되도록 인간이 추가하다

---

practice It is called a leap second that is added or subtracted.

mojo Extension or subtracting one second is called a leap second.

[tip] extension 늘이다 **subtract** 빼다 **leap** 건너 뛰다

is called a leap year 윤년이라 한다

---

practice The 2017 year is its 28th, and then how come is it happened?

[Suggestion] is it happened → does it happen

mojo The 2017 is 28th year of the occurrence happening. How come is it coming?

[tip] How come is it coming 어째서 발생하는 것일까?

text	정유년 새해가 시작되는 1월1일 아침 9시는 1초 늦게 시작된다.
try	
	[word] 새해 **new year** 늦게 시작된다 **start late**

text	8시 59분 59초에서 9시 정각이 되는 게 아니라 59분 60초, 즉 1초가 추가된 뒤 9시로 넘어간다.
try	
	[word] 정각 **just** ～아니라, ～이다 **it is not~, but~**

text	하루 한 바퀴 도는 지구의 자전이 밀물과 썰물, 지진, 화산 활동 등에 의해 미세하게 느려진 게 누적되면서, 항상 일정한 원자시계와 1초 가까운 오차가 발생해, 바로잡는 것이다.
try	
	[word] 자전 **rotation** 밀물과 썰물 **tide and ebb** 지진 **earthquake** 화산활동 **volcanic activity** 원자시계 **atomic clock** 오차 **an accidental error**

practice	When the 9 a.m. on January first of the New Year, ~~calling~~ the Chicken year in Chinese, will start one second late. **[Suggestion] New Year, calling the Chicken year → New Year, called the Chicken year**
mojo	The 9 a.m. of January first day of the new year, called 'the Chicken Year,' will start one second late. 9 a.m. on January 1st starting with the Chicken Year comes one minute late. **[tip] the Chicken year in Chinese 정유년 comes one minute late 일분 늦게 온다**

practice	It is not just 9 a.m. after 8 hour 59 minute 59 second, but will be 59 minute 60 second, that will be 9 hour following on second to add.
mojo	The 9 a.m. doesn't come after 8:59.59., but the 9 a.m. come following 8:60 after one second added to 8:59.59. **[tip] just · sharp · on the dot정각 follow 뒤이어 · 뒤따르다**

practice	With accumulating retarded fine times along with waves and tides, earthquake, volcanic activity when earth rotates round a day, a usual atomic clock causes an accidental error, it needs to correct.
mojo	With the earth rotation being minutely behind time and accumulated, caused by a rising tide and ebb, earthquake and volcanic activity, the errors in the range of onc second are unavoidable on the basis of atomic clock so the error is corrected in the process. **[tip] minutely 미세하게** **on the basis of atomic clock 항상 일정한 원자시계 · 기준이 되는 시계**

지난 1972년 이후 27차례에 걸쳐 1초씩 늘렸고 이번이 28번째 윤초다.

지난 1972년 **last 1972** 28번째 **twenty eighth**

practice

Since it has added one second 27 times after last 1972, this is 28th time leap second.

mojo

One second has been added 27 times since 1972, and 2017 is the 28th leap year.

[tip] since 그 후 · 이래 · 이후

✎

대자연을 누비는 로드 트립

미국 대도시를 여행한다면 대중교통이 편하다.

뉴욕·샌프란시스코·시애틀처럼 도시 안에서만 돌아다닌다면 그렇다.

그러나 그랜드 캐니언·옐로스톤·로키산 국립공원 같은 곳으로 간다면?

선택은 둘 중 하나다.

관광버스를 타는 단체 패키지 여행을 하거나 직접 자동차를 몰거나.

솔직히 정답은 이미 알고 있다.

일정에 쫓겨 전망대에서 기념사진 찍을 시간밖에 안주는 패키지 여행보다

직접 운전하는 로드트립을 해야

아메리카 대륙의 웅대한 자연을 제대로 즐길 수 있다는 사실을 말이다.

미국이든 캐나다든 북미 대륙에서는

서부지역이 자동차 여행을 즐기기에 좋다.

산맥협곡사막 빙하 등 대자연이 빚은 절경이

다채롭게 펼쳐지기 때문이다.

가령 샌프란시스코를 기점으로 삼아보자.

북쪽으로 가면 와이너리 (소노마·나파밸리)를 여행하고,

남쪽으로 가면 해변 드라이브 코스(퍼시픽 코스트 하이웨이)를 달리고,

동쪽으로 가면 요세미티 국립공원이 들어선 시애라 네바다 산맥을 만난다.

여행 방향을 어디로 잡느냐에 따라 전혀 다른 여행이 된다.

text	대자연을 누비는 로드 트립
try	

[word] 돌아다니다 · 유랑하다 rove

60

Mojo Writing

Road trip crisscrossing nature

The public transportation is more convenient to travel the U.S. metropolitans. It is right to say it only if we get around downtown cities like New York, San Francisco or Seattle. But when you head for the national park such as Grand Canyon, Yellowstone or Rocky Mountains?

The alternative choice is whether we leave on a package trip riding tourist bus or drive a car ourselves. We just know the answer: we can enjoy majestic and beautiful nature of the American continent enough when we drive a car on road trip, not ride a package trip in which only time is allowed for us to take pictures standing on the observatory being pressed for time.

The western area across the North America, whether it is the U.S. or Canada, is much ideal for car driving. It is just because the majestic sight out of the grand nature of mountains valley or glacier is spreading across the country suppose we set out from San Francisco. If we head for northern direction, we have a chance to get around the Sonoma or Napa Valley, and if we drive off in southerly direction, we can reach seaside drive course, the Pacific coast highway. If we take eastern direction, we come across Sierra Nevada Mountains, where the Yosemite National Park starts. Depending on where to take a direction, it could be a different travel.

practice	Road trip roving over great nature
mojo	**Road trip crisscrossing nature**

[tip] **crisscross** 누비다 · 교차하다 · 십자 · 종횡으로 움직이다 · 누비다

<table>
<tr><td>text</td><td>미국 대도시를 여행한다면 대중교통이 편하다.</td></tr>
<tr><td>try</td><td>[word] 대중교통 public transportation 대도시 big city</td></tr>
<tr><td>text</td><td>뉴욕 · 샌프란시스코 · 시애틀처럼 도시 안에서만 돌아다닌다면 그렇다.</td></tr>
<tr><td>try</td><td>[word] 도시 안에서 inside city</td></tr>
<tr><td>text</td><td>그러나 그랜드 캐니언 · 옐로스톤 · 로키산 국립공원 같은 곳으로 간다면?</td></tr>
<tr><td>try</td><td>[word] 그랜드 캐니언 Grand Canyon 옐로스톤 Yellowstone 로키산 Rocky Mountain</td></tr>
<tr><td>text</td><td>선택은 둘 중 하나다. 관광버스를 타는 단체 패키지 여행을 하거나 직접 자동차를 몰거나.</td></tr>
<tr><td>try</td><td>[word] 선택 choose 관광버스 tour bus 단체 여행 package tour</td></tr>
</table>

When you travel around big cities in U.S., public transportations are convenient.

mojo

The public transportation is more convenient to travel the U.S. metropolitans.

[tip] is more convenient to travel 여행하기 더 편하다

metropolitan 대도시 · 수도권

---

practice

It is ~~right saying as~~ the inside cities like New York, San Francisco and Seattle.

[Suggestion] It is right saying as → It is right to say as you go around

mojo

It is right to say it only if we get around downtown cities like New York, San Francisco or Seattle.

[tip] it is right to say 말하는 것이 맞다 **onlyif** 해야만 **get around** 돌아다니다

---

practice

But when you head for the national park, such as Grand Canyon, Yellowstone and Rocky Mountain, how does it?

mojo

But when you head for the national park such as Grand Canyon, Yellowstone or Rocky Mountains?

[tip] Mountains 산맥 **headfor** 향하다 · 나아가다

---

practice

Choice is one of two ways. One is package tour by a tourist bus or the other is driving one's own car to go.

mojo

The alternative choice is whether we leave on a package trip riding tourist bus or drive a car ourselves.

[tip] alternative ~ whether 이거든 저거든 양자택일

text	솔직히 정답은 이미 알고 있다. 일정에 쫓겨 전망대에서 기념사진 찍을 시간밖에 안주는 패키지 여행보다 직접 운전하는 로드트립을 해야 아메리카 대륙의 웅대한 자연을 제대로 즐길 수 있다는 사실을 말이다.
try	
	[word] 솔직히 **to be honest · frankly** 일정 **schedule** 전망대 **observation deck** 웅대한 **great** 제대로 **fully**

text	미국이든 캐나다든 북미 대륙에서는 서부지역이 자동차 여행을 즐기기에 좋다.
try	[word] 서부지역 **the western part**

text	빙하 등 대자연이 빚은 절경이 다채롭게 펼쳐지기 때문이다.
try	[word] 빙하 **glacier** 빚은 **create** 절경 **superb view** 다채롭다 **colorful** 펼쳐지다 **expand**

<table>
<tr><td>practice</td><td>We already know the answer to be honest. It is true that driving oneself for going road trip can enjoy fully around grand nature in American continent than package tour which is allowed short time at observation deck for taking memorial pictures along with limited schedule.</td></tr>
<tr><td>mojo</td><td>We just know the answer: we can enjoy majestic and beautiful nature of the American continent enough when we drive a car on road trip, not ride a package trip in which only time is allowed for us to take pictures standing on the observatory being pressed for time.
[tip] majestic and beautiful nature 장엄하고 아름다운 자연
being pressed for time 시간일정에 쫓겨</td></tr>
<tr><td>practice</td><td><s>In North America either the U.S. or Canada,</s> the western part is good for car driving.
[Suggestion] In North America either the U.S. or Canada, → Either the US or Canada in North America,</td></tr>
<tr><td>mojo</td><td>The western area across the North America, whether it is the U.S. or Canada, is much ideal for car driving.
[tip] across 걸쳐서 whether it is the US or Canada 미국이든 캐나다든
ideal · perfect 이상적</td></tr>
<tr><td>practice</td><td>It is because that both glacier and superb view created by grand nature are expanded colorfully.</td></tr>
<tr><td>mojo</td><td>It is just because the majestic sight out of the grand nature of mountains, valleys or glaciers is spreading across the country.
[tip] it is just because 바로 이렇기 때문이다 spread 펼치다</td></tr>
</table>

| text | 가령 샌프란시스코를 기점으로 삼아보자. |

| try | [word] 기점 **the starting point** |

| text | 북쪽으로 가면 와이너리 (소노마 · 나파밸리)를 여행하고, 남쪽으로 가면 해변 드라이브 코스(퍼시픽 코스트 하이웨이)를 달리고, 동쪽으로 가면 요세미티 국립공원이 들어선 시애라 네바다 산맥을 만난다. |

| try | [word] 와이너리 **winery(Sonoma/Napa valley)** 퍼시픽 코스트 하이웨이 **Pacific Coast Highway** 요세미티 **Yosemite National Park** 시에라 네바다 **Sierra Nevada** |

| text | 여행 방향을 어디로 잡느냐에 따라 전혀 다른 여행이 된다. |

| try | [word] ~에 따라 **depend on** |

| **practice** | Let's make San Francisco as a starting point. |
| **mojo** | Suppose we set out from San Francisco. |

Suppose we set out from San Francisco.

[tip] **suppose** 가정하다 · 예정이다

---

practice

If you head for North, you go to tour Nonoma or Napa valley winery, for South you can run on the Pacific Coast Highway, for East you face at Sierra Nevada Mount located the Yosemite National Park.

mojo

If we head for northern direction, we have a chance to get around the Sonoma or Napa Valley, and if we drive off in southerly direction, we can reach seaside drive course, the Pacific coast highway. If we take eastern direction, we come across Sierra Nevada Mountains, where the Yosemite National Park starts.

[tip] **drive off** 달려가다 **southerly** 남쪽으로 향하는 · 남풍

come across 우연히 만나다

---

practice

~~Depend on~~ where you get a direction, it could be different travel.

[Suggestion] **depend on** → **depending on**

mojo

Depending on where to take a direction, it could be a different travel.

[tip] **Where to take** · **where you take** 방향을 어디로 잡느냐

모조 영작

초판 1쇄 인쇄 2017년 4월 14일
초판 1쇄 발행 2017년 4월 21일

지은이 토마스 안 · 벨라 정
펴낸곳 이런타임(elearntime)

주소 서울시 종로구 삼봉로 95 2-1004(견지동 대성스카이렉스)
전화 02-739-5333
팩스 02-739-5777
e-mail elearntime@naver.com

ISBN 979-11-85345-11-6 13740

모조 영작
Mojo English Writing